UNBUILT
CLEMSON

DENNIS S. TAYLOR

FOREWORD BY GERALD VANDER MEY

ISBN: 978-1-949979-62-6

Published by Clemson University Press.
For information about our publishing program,
visit our website www.clemson.edu/press.

Designed by Lindsay Scott

CONTENTS

LIST OF ABBREVIATIONS

a — accession

b — box

BAR — Board of Architectural Review

CAAH — College of Arts, Architecture and Humanities

CAC.C — Clemson Architecture Center in Charleston

CEC — Continuing Education Center

CFC — Commission on the Future of Clemson University

CMP — Cresap, McCormick and Paget Management Consultants

CUF — Clemson University Foundation

CU-ICAR — Clemson University International Center for Automotive Research

CULSC&A — Clemson University Libraries Special Collections and Archives

CVA — Center for Visual Arts

f — folder

FAIA — Fellow of the American Institute of Architects

KVA — Kennedy and Violich Architecture, Ltd.

LEED — Leadership in Energy and Environmental Design

MSS — Manuscript collection

PSHKD — Perry, Shaw and Hepburn, Kehoe and Dean

S — Series in the Clemson University Archives

THS — *The High Seminary*

USGBC — United States Green Building Council

WPA — Works Project Administration

LIST OF FIGURES

FOREWORD

THE SPARK OF AN IDEA FOR A NEW PROJECT IS A WONDERFUL THING. At its best, it can energize a whole organization to put their best efforts into realizing a vision. Road blocks can be swept aside, resources can be found, and energy and enthusiasm can be boundless. Optimally, the spark stays bright and shines all the way through to the ribbon cutting. The reality, however, is that the project development process takes years and encounters many challenges along the way. The kernel of the principal idea often evolves along with support and resources; sometimes the project gets sidetracked and sometimes it never reaches official status as a true project. Other times, the project can have what appears to be a clear path to realization, only to get hit with an unanticipated obstacle that cannot be overcome.

Every project has its associated risks. The very idea of creating a new facility or renovating an existing one has inherent unknowns that can be major disruptors. External or internal required approvals, leadership changes, priority modifications, contractor issues, high bids, design complexities, natural disasters, and other factors can singly or collectively derail a project or change it in significant ways.

There are many different types of capital projects associated with higher education institutions such as classroom or office buildings, residence halls, and athletic venues. Most Clemson University projects are born out of an essential need. Enrollment and program growth are key drivers, but stewardship also plays an important role. Over the last thirty years, the university's total enrollment has grown from 12,000 students to more than 24,000, a doubling that requires significant accommodations for teaching, research, student housing, student life, and other associated needs. In anticipation of this growth, and in some cases in response to it, the campus and its satellite facilities have grown by more than two million square feet through more than sixty major capital projects

and $1.4 billion in investment. About half of all major projects are renovations. These can be comprehensive in nature, as evidenced by the rebuild of Hardin Hall on the Clemson campus. Projects can also be much less visible, such as the air conditioning renovation of a major facility. Even these kinds of projects face substantial risk. In the case of Hardin Hall, for example, rebuilding was delayed by nearly a year over a debate with external agencies concerning the nature of the renovation, and the project very nearly went unrealized.

The launch of a major capital project can be a complex process. Often it takes years of preparation to gain alignment regarding program, cost, schedule, funding, site, and other characteristics. Projects normally begin as a focused conversation that targets a specific need that can be addressed by a major project. For example, growing numbers of first-year students who are required to live on campus create the need for a new facility. If this need is substantiated by long-range planning, conversations with the office of admissions, supporting data, and financial projections, the project could find itself on a list for funding consideration. If the need is identified in the *Long-Range Framework Plan*, a significant level of legitimacy is demonstrated.[1]

The project development process is fundamentally linear. First, there are internal approvals that must be engaged through a pre-concept plan. The concept, if approved, leads to a feasibility study. If favorable, the feasibility study can lead to a discussion about priorities and potential funding. This discussion can lead to a set of first-level executive and state approvals. Planning and design can begin once these approvals are put in place, and if the outcome is in reasonable alignment with initial goals and funding, the project can proceed to second-level of executive and state approvals. Each of these steps represent significant challenges to the achievement of a project. At any point in the process, a project can be propelled forward, stalled, recast, or rejected. Once the second round of approvals is in place, most of the hurdles have been cleared and the hard work of implementing the plan begins.

It is a worthwhile exercise to look back on projects that have gone unrealized. It holds a mirror up to the subject that allows us to consider what may have been, and to examine from a distance the value and importance of the divergence. Upon reflection, it may be useful to think of some of these projects as "unbuilt for now." We should keep these projects in the back of our minds in a way that may offer the opportunity to REKINDLE SOME OF THE IDEAS THAT FIRST BROUGHT THE PROJECTS FORWARD.

GERALD VANDER MEY

DIRECTOR, UNIVERSITY PLANNING AND DESIGN
2020

INTRODUCTION

"UNBUILT" SUGGESTS A NEGATIVE OR OPPOSING FORCE OR ACTION. When used to describe architecture, infrastructure, or art, it arouses curiosity and speculation, with a hint of mystery. Literature, both popular and scholarly, as well as online resources such as websites and blogs, are replete with studies of unbuilt buildings, dams, highways, monuments, and cities, all intriguingly described as vanished, zombie, ghostly, visionary, or forgotten. Such writings appeared in Europe as early as 1925 with the publication of Josef Ponten's *Architektur die Nicht Gebaut Werde* (*Architecture That Is Not Built*), but nothing similar appeared in the United States until the publication of Alison Sky and Michelle Stone's *Unbuilt America* in 1976. That work first treated the subject comprehensively by examining "forgotten architecture" from the Jeffersonian period to the space age; it focused on "realizable architecture," rather than fantasy or utopian plans for buildings and monuments, or "monstrosities" and rejected competition entries. *Unbuilt Clemson* takes a similar approach, with slight modifications.

Unbuilt Clemson documents the history of a variety of projects planned for the campus but never constructed. It synthesizes information contained in disparate primary sources (most found in the Clemson University Library Archives & Special Collections, CULSC&A) into a single source that allows readers to discover sixteen projects—each with a story of the past, but also relevant to today. The projects, seen through the lens of campus development, will take on additional meaning if the reader possesses a nodding acquaintance with Clemson's history—particularly milestones like World War II, the admission of women, racial integration, acquisition of university status, and athletic championships. Readers should also be aware of two terms from the argot of unbuilt architecture, which differs from that of realized architecture. *Visionary unbuilt* denotes

schemes that invite a forward glance to an ideal or better tomorrow, while *contingent unbuilt* denotes those that invite a backward glance along the multiple routes history might have taken.[1]

These distinctions, visionary and contingent, act as keys that open the past, present, and future to alternative visions and narratives. This approach, also known as virtual history, is predicated on the counterfactual, or, what might have been.[2] Virtual history encourages the reader to ask "what if?"—not interpreted as "what would the campus have looked like if the projects were constructed?" but rather "would the history of Clemson University be altered if the projects had been constructed?" *Unbuilt Clemson* does not furnish all of the answers, but instead encourages readers to engage in this unconventional mental exercise in an unconventional way.[3] Such thinking does not grant one permission to discount history or abandon fact, however; quite the opposite. The historian's quest is not to determine what must or might have happened, but rather what the evidence obliges us to conclude took place.[4] The evidence, presented here in vignettes, portrays individuals and groups whose affection for Clemson birthed visions that have not dimmed with time, but grow brighter and more compelling with its passage. Some of those visionaries have reputations known only to a limited audience, while others have garnered accolades, but are worthy of more; all deserve recognition for their innovative, imaginative, and sometimes edgy designs.

Not all of the unbuilt projects included here are buildings, however. Many will be surprised to learn of a planned railroad that would have linked the campus directly to the train station at Calhoun, bisecting what is today downtown Clemson. Other gems of the campus's virtual history include a new entrance to the campus that bypassed the traditional entry to Fort Hill, the home of Thomas and Anna Clemson; an arboretum that would have turned the entire central campus into an Edenic woodland; a historic preservation district with numerous architecturally significant buildings; a living history farm village of the early 1800s (similar to Colonial Williamsburg) on the present site of Lee and Lowry Halls; and a research community of undergraduates and retirees, accessible only by water taxi. These and other projects went unbuilt for numerous reasons, but often because pressing needs or competing priorities, which the Trustees judged as more necessary, superseded them. That body, and those who held the office of President, navigated internal and external obstacles—politics, the occasional personality clash, the 1918 pandemic, global wars, impending inundation of campus lands, and economic depressions and recessions—to grow and advance the institution.

Thanks to the advent of sophisticated planning in the form of commissioned master plans and a new organizational structure that emphasized campus development, following World War II progress and modernization went hand in hand. But the phenomenal building program made possible by state funding also had a downside. Projects—and growth—were tethered to state funds, which were stretched to the max. As a result, some exemplary designs for modernization fell victim to unalterable budgets that neither the state nor the University could augment. Those unbuilt projects yielded an important takeaway, however; state funding alone could no longer support building construction at all of South Carolina's institutions of higher education. Other methods were needed to compensate for the loss, and Trustees focused their efforts on forming partnerships with various entities, creatively addressing the challenge of building construction by allying with local government, business, industry, and notable individuals. Successful partnerships produced successful projects, while partnerships that failed to

coalesce, though sparked by vision and thoughtful planning, never took physical form.

The projects discussed in this book cover three chronological periods: the years before the advent of modern campus planning, 1890–1947; the period of modernization, which saw the creation of several professional master plans, 1947–89; and the most recent period, characterized by partnerships, beginning in the 1990s. The study ends in 2014—a logical endpoint, as the university had just embarked on a new campus master plan. Completed in 2017, it stands as an outstanding example of modern campus master planning, beckoning all who are interested to glimpse the Clemson University campus of the future. For readers who wish to examine sources cited in this work and held by the Clemson University Archives, they may find the notes and bibliography useful for details concerning access; however, unique identifiers could not always be provided for specific items because physical processing and cataloging of some collections was underway as THIS BOOK TOOK FINAL FORM.

CHAPTER ONE

PRESSING NEEDS. COMPETING PRIORITIES

1890–1947

FIG. 1–1 *Fort Hill Property Map*

FROM ITS FOUNDING, the growth and development of the Clemson College campus went hand in hand. The original 814-acre Clemson campus expanded gradually toward the towns of Calhoun, Central, and Pendleton, South Carolina, growing by another 22,000 acres when reclaimed forest lands were acquired in the 1930s. The physical plant developed just as progressively, though somewhat sporadically. There were growth spurts—the first when the college was founded, another during the Great Depression, and once more following the end of World War II. Various factors contributed to this growth and development: topography, climate, natural disasters, politics, philanthropy, and fluctuating economic conditions. But the Board of Trustees, mindful of the vision of Thomas Green Clemson, shepherded growth and development; ultimately, they determined what was built and what was not.

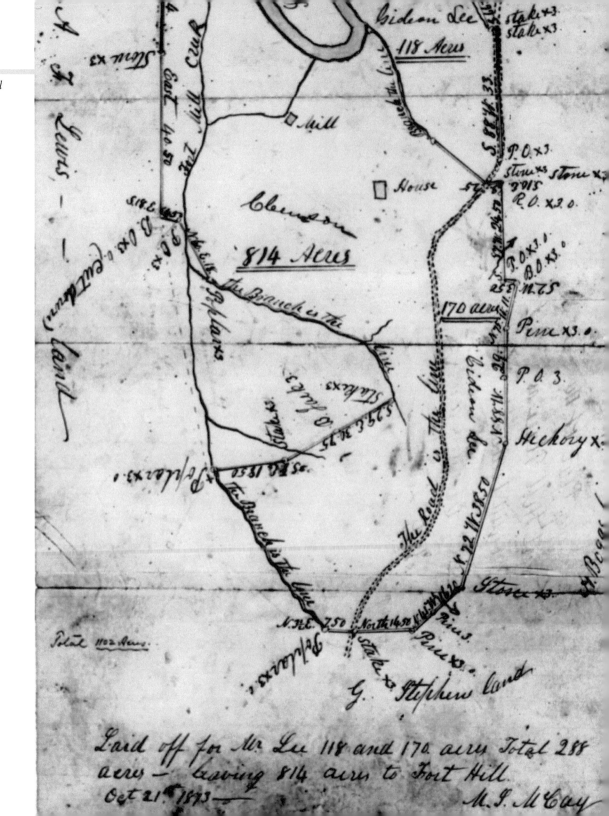

The actions of the first Board of Trustees established precedents for future planning and construction by assigning the President a pivotal role. After visiting the campuses of institutions in neighboring states and deciding that some twenty buildings were required for Clemson,[1] the Trustees hired the Atlanta architectural firm of Bruce and Morgan to design them.[2] To execute the grand Collegiate Gothic designs, the Trustees "realized the necessity of having some competent person . . . to overlook and plan the work . . . and to arrange and locate the buildings . . . and entrust him with these duties."[3] That individual—Henry A. Strode, the university's first President—possessed experience and ability as an administrator and educator, but not as a builder. However, with the assistance of an on-site junior architect and building supervisor hired by Bruce and Morgan,[4] Strode carried out his duties as "President-contractor" conscientiously

and with minimal complaints. His few letters to Board President Richard Wright Simpson described difficulties in procuring building materials and labor, and conveyed his impatience with the Trustees' decision regarding the location of the Main Building, which they had exempted from the original charge.[5] After Simpson informed Strode that it "would be situated . . . at the top of the hill near the Calhoun residence [Fort Hill],"[6] Strode, most likely with the assistance of Bruce and Morgan's attaché, arranged the other buildings on a long north-south axis behind the Main Building. He placed the Chemistry Building (now Hardin Hall) farther down across from the eastern facade of Fort Hill[7] (the Clemson homestead that stood in almost the exact center of campus); other farm structures such as barns, siloes, sheds, and cow houses in the surrounding countryside completed the bucolic landscape.

By the end of October 1891, only three of the buildings enumerated by the Trustees in 1890 were still in progress: the infirmary, the chapel, and the Main Building.[8] A facility for athletics, understood by most as a gymnasium, did not appear on the list of completed or in-progress structures for more than another decade. It became, therefore, one of Clemson's first "unbuilt" projects,[9] owing to other pressing needs but also to a prevailing view that sports were played outdoors and did not require a building.[10] But in his report in 1900 President Hartzog chided Trustees about the need to construct a gymnasium: "Football and baseball are excellent games," he wrote, "but not more than one-fourth of the students in the colleges take part in these exercises. . . . Military drills cannot take the place of athletic exercises."[11] His position gained the support of the Board of Visitors, an independent body of citizens appointed by the Board to recommend improvements, three years later:

> We were surprised to find the college without a gymnasium. There is no organized or systematic physical culture required of the students except such as is incident to the drill. Those who take any such exercise do so in a desultory way in their quarters and without the aid of scientific instruction and direction. . . . A gymnasium properly equipped and under the direction of a competent instructor has come to be considered a necessary adjunct to all first class modern colleges. We recommend by all means the building of a gymnasium as soon as possible. . . . Every student, not physically incapacitated, should be required to take the gymnasium course.[12]

Their findings prompted the creation of a small makeshift gym in one wing of Agricultural Hall (now Sikes Hall) when it was completed in 1904, but a small gymnasium, in Holtzendorff Hall, was not built until 1916, and a gymnasium with seating did not appear until 1930.[13] A formal architectural rendering of a gym might have generated support and ensured an earlier completion, but would have entailed employing the services of an architect and contractor—expenses the Executive Committee would not have approved.

The Executive Committee approved building projects if money was available to finance their construction *and* if they were needed; if money was not available, projects did not happen. The College's budget depended upon several sources of revenue—interest from the Clemson bequest, the Morrill Land Grant endowment, the Hatch Act of 1887, a modest annual appropriation from the state of South Carolina, tuition, and revenue from the tax on fertilizers, which fluctuated yearly.[14] These were either allocated for specific purposes or used for daily operations, all high priorities which did not include campus planning. Cadet discipline and the challenges of running the fledgling college[15] outweighed other undertakings, as Strode and his immediate successors Presidents Edwin B. Craighead, Mark Bernard Hardin, Henry S. Hartzog, and Patrick H. Mell discovered soon after taking office. For instance, President Mell (1902–10) attempted to develop the campus twice—once with a project he inherited, and a later project he instigated; NEITHER CAME TO FRUITION.

RAIL LINE TO CALHOUN

1899–1908

ELL'S FIRST PROJECT as President, which began late in the administration of President Hartzog, would have built a railroad line from the campus to the town of Calhoun, a stop on the rail line of the Atlanta and Charlotte Air Line.[16] The project originated from Act No. 33 of the South Carolina General Assembly in 1900; it granted permission to Clemson to link the coal chute at Mechanical Hall (present site of Rhodes Hall) to Calhoun Station, just over a mile away, for the purpose of hauling coal and other supplies. The rail line would have begun at Mechanical Hall, passed to the rear of Fort Hill, past the rear of the barracks, to Sloan's store, past Kellar's [sic; Judge Keller's General Merchandise Store], and then to the train depot.[17]

Plan of Clemson College Railway.

Scale, 200 feet per inch.

FIG. 1-3 *Calhoun Rail Line Blueprint*

The Trustees authorized outgoing President Hartzog and Trustee R. E. Bowen to secure a written agreement regarding the railroad and its operation, directed Professor P. T. Brodie to perform a survey (which was accepted by rail authorities), and appointed Trustees Benjamin Tillman, Daniel Keating Norris, and Simpson to interview landowners and secure rights of way.[18] The project also gained support from Engineering Professor Walter Riggs, who judged its construction necessary for a projected power plant and desirable for instruction:

> We should establish an electric line to Calhoun not only for hauling purposes but to give to our students instruction in Electric Street Railway Engineering [sic]. The electric street railway is the most important branch of the entire electrical industry, and yet no college in the country gives this practical engineering course. It is an opportunity for Clemson that will, I hope, in the near future be appreciated and embraced by our trustees.[19]

The minutes recorded no further details of the project until December 1908, when the Trustees and President Mell authorized Riggs to study the feasibility of the project and develop an estimate of the cost. Riggs's report, which indicated the approach he would later apply to budget issues and construction once he became President, considered only freight haulage, not passenger service, which many wanted. He thoroughly analyzed the volume of coal hauled, the cost of constructing the line, the potential cost savings, and the project's suitability as an investment and concluded his report by stating that the project "was not recommended from a business standpoint."[20] The Trustees, apparently satisfied with Riggs's conclusions, took no further action.

Had the Trustees approved construction of this rail line, Clemson College and the town of Clemson would have developed in vastly different ways. The topography of the land between the terminal points would have made necessary the construction of a trestle or other elevated rail line, and that structure would have impacted both commercial and residential sections of the towns of Clemson and Calhoun. If only for the sake of convenience in hauling coal and supplies from Calhoun to the campus, the rail line would have been a success. Moreover, it would have allowed construction of a new power plant to begin two decades earlier, and, although it was intended to haul only coal, the line would no doubt have eventually shuttled town and gown passengers to and from the train depot. But perhaps the most exciting consequence of constructing the rail line—affording students the opportunity to study electrical engineering in 1900—would have led to an innovative engineering curriculum rivaling those of Cornell University and the Massachusetts Institute of Technology, BOTH OUTSTANDING LEADERS IN THE EMERGING FIELD.

PRESIDENT MELL'S SECOND foray into campus development occurred when he sought to employ a professional landscape architect to improve the campus. But when Trustees Tillman and John Wannamaker intervened, his effort turned into a saga of personalities and egos that played out over five years. Of the three men Mell, educated as a geologist and botanist with a distinctive record of publications on plants and climates, had most thoughtfully considered ways to improve the campus landscape.

CAMPUS LANDSCAPING

JEDBURG EXPERIMENT STATION

1902–1908

But Tillman, the Trustee who hired Mell and understood local plant varieties and landscaping problems unique to the southern climate (and who had selected specific plants and shrubs for campus plantings), zealously guarded college expenditures. The other Trustee, Wannamaker, chaired the Experiment Station committee and supported campus improvements, especially those at the new 300-acre Jedburg Experiment Station near Summerville; he believed expansion of the physical plant was essential for Clemson to carry out its mission and that hiring a professional landscaper would accomplish both objectives. Complicating matters further were the prospective hires: George Amos Parker and Harlan Page Kelsey.

FIG. 1-4
President Mell

9

FIG. 1-5 *Parker*

Sometime in 1903, Parker, a noted landscape architect in Hartford, Connecticut, visited Clemson to survey the campus and make recommendations on its development. Exactly who invited Parker initially is not clear, but after Mell became President in the fall of 1902 he resumed the dialogue with Parker and invited him back "to go at this work of improvement in an intelligent and systematic way."[21] The New Hampshire-born Parker enjoyed a reputation as a leader in the American Civic Association and as a progressive force in park designs that featured areas for baseball and other recreational activities, but also for specific age and gender groups.[22] Parker offered his services free of charge and, most likely as an act of reciprocity, accepted Mell's invitation to speak on the subject of "development of public roads in cities and villages" at a Famer's Institute at Clemson in August 1904.[23] Parker then produced a general plan with maps and specifications that identified areas on campus in need of improvement, although these areas were never clearly identified.[24] After completing the project's first phase, which called for grading around the Textile Building (now Godfrey Hall), Parker planned to implement the next phase of his plans, but illness and a heavy workload in Hartford prevented him from traveling. Instead, he recommended his colleague, Kelsey, to perform the work.[25]

FIG. 1.6 *Kelsey*

A native of Kansas, Kelsey grew up in Highlands, North Carolina and spent most of his professional career in the southeastern United States as a nurseryman and botanist. After mediocre success in establishing an arboretum in Highlands and a planned community, New Holland, at Lake Mattamuskeet, North Carolina, Kelsey moved to Boston in 1896 and started a nursery in nearby Salem, Massachusetts.[26] There Kelsey partnered with architect Irving Guild to complete various landscaping projects on the east coast.[27]

The following year, Kelsey returned south when textile mill founder Thomas Fleming Parker hired him to lay out the grounds of his new Monaghan Mill in Greenville.[28] Kelsey's work there served as a launch pad for work elsewhere in the state and soon he became the standard bearer of the City Beautiful movement in South Carolina. In that role, he crusaded for voluntarism as an avenue to civic improvement, for example, assisting women in Rock Hill to organize a local association in 1904, and, that same year, lecturing on civic improvement at the State House in Columbia.[29] Kelsey spoke against billboards, hackberry trees, and telephone poles to convey his belief that design could not be separated from social issues, civic pride, and engagement. His following included city leaders in Marion, Columbia, and Greenville, all of whom responded to his message by hiring him to create civic improvement plans.[30]

Trustees Wannamaker and Tillman held opposing views about hiring Kelsey. Wannamaker approved, but Tillman, who objected for reasons of cost, directed Mell to implement some of Parker's plans until he was able to travel again.[31] Mell honored Tillman's directive, although the records do not indicate exactly what he accomplished. After a year passed with Parker still unable to travel, however, Mell turned to Wannamaker and D. B. Johnson, president of Winthrop College in Rock Hill (who had also contracted with Kelsey) for advice; both recommended Kelsey. Mell then contacted Kelsey about taking up Parker's work[32] and Kelsey answered affirmatively with an outline of his charges, expressing great enthusiasm for creating an arboretum at Clemson.[33] Mell, however, downplayed the arboretum and focused on cost; he made it clear that Parker had done his work "as a labor of love" and without charge.[34] Dissatisfied with the reply Kelsey sent, Mell attempted again to persuade Parker to undertake the work at Clemson, but without success. The following year, Mell went back to Kelsey with a clear statement of his objective:

> I would be very glad, therefore, to know what you will charge the college to take the entire Campus [sic], consisting of something over one hundred acres, and place the same in a beautiful condition. . . . We can furnish all the labor to do all of the necessary work under your direction in the shape of grading, setting out grass, and planting trees and shrubs. We have naturally a very beautiful spot, sufficiently rolling to give it variety, and there is a native growth of oaks and other trees and a fair starting of grass. . . . There is needed, however, the touch of a skillful hand to give the grounds a finished appearance that is so attractive in parks all over the country. We have a number of large buildings distributed through the grounds and the faculty have their homes about the campus.[35]

FIG. 1-7 *Original Entrance, 1900*

Kelsey replied that Mell's proposition would take two or three years to accomplish and could not be done with a plan "worked out in one or two visits," but agreed to undertake the work of 125 acres at eight dollars per acre over three years.[36] Kelsey arrived in Clemson in December 1907, toured the campus with Mell, and discussed the work, focusing on the grading near the Textile Building and a change in the main approach road from the Main Building past the Agricultural Hall to create a new entrance over the hill where the Clemson College Hotel stood.[37] Mell, while pleased with Kelsey's recommendations, expressed concern to Wannamaker that Kelsey "might suggest some radical changes" which he feared the Board of Trustees would not accede to; nevertheless he believed Kelsey's plans could be carried out without difficulty.[38] Those plans included enlisting the help of professors and students to collect the data Kelsey required, producing a topographic map of the main campus, and, to secure Wannamaker's support, laying out the grounds at Jedburg.[39]

Tillman, upon learning from Wannamaker of Mell's intent to hire Kelsey, expressed again his "unalterable" opposition to hiring Kelsey "or anyone else" and countered that "Burkmann [sic] of Augusta, or some other landscape architect" would produce a plan more cheaply.[40] To placate Tillman, Mell wrote George Parker and pleaded with him to return and finish the work he had begun in 1904,[41] but Parker would not budge and replied to Mell's groveling with a five-page declination. Although he "strongly desired to be involved with the preservation and interpretation of the grounds of Fort Hill," which he called "a most loved spot for the people," on a campus that he believed would become "a masterpiece of landscape art with far reaching influence," poor health had made him unable to work and travel south again. He recommended Kelsey for the second time, because of "his youth, superior education and artistic temperament," which he had observed when he and Kelsey had reviewed the plans for Clemson. Parker concluded that his work at Clemson College, which he summed up as "a bright spot in my life and . . . and among my most pleasant memories . . . is ended."[42]

With Parker's definitive response, Wannamaker, who wanted to "hurry and hire Kelsey" so work at the Jedburg Station could commence, instructed Mell to obtain the plans and contracts from Kelsey for review by the Trustees. Mell complied, but at their next meeting in Columbia the Trustees refused to sign a contract with Kelsey, or to buy his plans outright, offering instead to pay him on a per-visit basis—something Kelsey, ever the savvy businessman, shunned.[43] Mell, who no doubt felt chagrined by the Board's decision, later lamented to Wannamaker "all of these plans were knocked to pieces and I was left suspended in the air" over Tillman's unwillingness to pay what Mell considered a minimal cost to improve the campus and begin the Station work.[44] Mell informed Kelsey of the Trustees' decision and, when he did not receive a response, concluded that

Kelsey was "deeply offended."[45] Mell quite likely misinterpreted Kelsey's reaction, however; Kelsey's demanding schedule included activities related to his nursery in Salem, his work with Guild, the Appalachian Forest Reserve, and his leadership of the American Civic Association and the Appalachian Mountain Club, all of which afforded him little time to brood over failing to acquire Clemson College as a new client. In 1910, after dissolving his partnership with Guild, Kelsey launched a new and successful business venture called The Highlands Nursery (named for his beloved Highlands, North Carolina), in Boxford, Massachusetts.[46]

Thus, the planning for campus development conceived by the triumvirate of Mell, Tillman, and Wannamaker and charted by landscape architects Parker and Kelsey, ended. For the short term, the failure to hire professional landscape architects halted efforts to develop an expansive green space around Fort Hill, with the entrance to campus from the ridge opposite Bowman Field. The work at the Jedburg Station, though delayed, was eventually completed.[47] In the long term, however, not hiring a professional landscape architect represented a lost opportunity to develop the campus in a thoughtful, systematic way; many years passed before landscape planning became a requisite part of campus master planning. The episode diminished the contribution of the President in campus development and illustrated the degree of control some of the Trustees exercised over what would be considered routine personnel matters today. President Mell became embroiled in the events surrounding the cadet walkout of April 1908 and found no more time to pursue further campus improvement; his presidency soon ended in discord. However his successor, the erstwhile Professor Riggs, adopted a much DIFFERENT AND DYNAMIC APPROACH TO CAMPUS DEVELOPMENT.

The Riggs presidency marked the first of three administrations to successfully carry out their envisioned building programs. In contrast to the previous aborted efforts, building projects in the decades that followed met with some resounding successes, but also a few failures. Presidents Riggs, W. E. Sikes, and, to a lesser degree, Robert Franklin Poole—each assisted by architect Rudolph Lee—spearheaded campus building during the period 1940–48 and pushed numerous projects through to completion. With each administration, the personal philosophies and visions of both the Presidents and the Trustees influenced the approach to campus development and determined the outcomes.

Riggs had clear a vision for the campus and expressed it early in his presidency. In a letter to the College community in March 1914 he revealed a ten-year plan:

> The present athletic field will be leveled with the earth obtained by removing the segment of the hill on the Hotel side of the field, and it will be converted into a formal garden of great beauty. The space below the track will be made into a sunken garden. It will be bounded by a stone wall five or six feet high opposite Robertson's store, with massive columns on each side of the road forming an entrance to the College grounds. The hill in front of the Textile School will be graded off to supply the earth for the high terrace in front of the Gymnasium. This terrace will have steps in front leading down to the sunken garden. The road that now crosses just behind the Textile Building will be relocated and will cross just behind the Gymnasium. The Trustee House will be torn down to open up a view of the Mansion from the campus and to get it out from

in front of the YMCA building and a John C. Calhoun Library which will stand between the Engineering Building and the Mansion. The Experiment Station greenhouse now in the middle of the campus will be located in connection with a $30,000 horticultural building that will occupy the site on which Col. Harden's house now stands. Between the Dairy building and Prof. Furman's residence will be built a $20,000 Farm Machinery building. On the lot next to Dr. Redfern's residence, unless the present hospital burns, or is torn down, will be built a modern hospital costing not less than $15,000. The grounds surrounding the Calhoun Mansion will be carefully laid out and the Mansion . . . turned into a relic . . . open at all times to students and visitors. [48]

From his experience as a professor, Riggs understood the limitations of the college budget and state funding. He anticipated the difficulty in financing future projects:

> Ten years is a long span in the life of an individual, but a very short period in the history of a College. The future of Clemson College ten years from now is but the writer's vision of what he thinks **should be** [sic]. It is as much the expression of a hope as a belief, because between him and the fulfillment of his vision lie the vicissitudes of financial support.[49]

He concluded his projections by asking: "Is this Clemson College of ten years from now an impossible dream? Not at all. In 1924 Clemson College will still not be complete. Growth is the law of life and never so long as the College is efficient will it become stationary."[50]

WALTER M. RIGGS

A eulogist at the memorial service of Walter Riggs compared him to Sir Christopher Wren, the famous English architect of the eighteenth century who rebuilt the city of London after the Great Fire of 1666:

> . . . standing at any point in the vicinity of Clemson College, we might equally well say of Dr. Riggs "If you seek his monument, look about you." For all, except the earliest, of the college buildings bear the imprint of his hands. Many an aspect of the campus is what it is because he built it or planted it or laid it out.[51]

In his early years as professor Riggs assisted in the construction of numerous buildings and agricultural structures on campus: the power station, barracks, experiment station, greenhouse, sidewalks, and water supply and heating systems in various buildings. Riggs actively participated in the life of the college and demonstrated his versatility by singing in the glee club, organizing the first football team, and promoting the playing of other sports—all of them requiring facilities to permit competition with other southern colleges.

As President of Clemson College, Riggs prioritized campus development projects and formulated lists for submission to state government for funding. He introduced the department of architectural studies and named Rudolph Lee as college architect in 1911; the two men worked to complete several campus buildings that were part of a building program that Riggs saw as essential to the continuance of the institution. As demonstration of his personal commitment to campus development, when funding fell short to complete the new YMCA Building in 1916, Riggs himself contributed a substantial sum.

TEN YEAR BUILDING PROGRAM

THE CLEMSON AGRICULTURAL COLLEGE.

1924-1934.

Buildings.	Approximate Cost.
1 — Dormitories (3) (for 600)	$ 325,000.00
2 — Gymnasium	150,000.00
3 — Hospital	75,000.00
Library	75,000.00
Live Stock Pavilion	15,000.00
Physics Building	75,000.00
Horticultural & Extension Building	50,000.00
Additions to Textile Building	150,000.00
Agricultural Hall Addition	35,000.00
4 Chapel Addition	35,000.00
∨ Messhall Addition	25,000.00
Greenhouse	5,000.00
Engineering Building Addition	150,000.00
Shop Buildings	50,000.00
Addition, Chemistry Building	50,000.00
Two miles hard surface road	60,000.00
Major additional equipment	50,000.00
Total	$1,375,000.00

(Above program provides for estimated attendance of 1,500)

(Apt.house for Faculty-   125,000.00

                                    $ 1,500,000.00

A man of action as well as vision, Riggs's personality and workaholic temperament help to explain both his many accomplishments and his early death.[52] As a professor and in the early years of his presidency, Riggs thrust himself into construction projects and earned himself the nickname "Bull."[53] He labored alongside college workers to construct barns and similar outbuildings, and also supervised convicts as they constructed cement sidewalks to connect campus buildings. "We have a definite plan that we are working to," he wrote the Trustees, "which, when completed, even if it takes years, will greatly enhance the appearance of our grounds."[54] Part of that plan—naming Rudolph Lee as the college architect in 1911—enabled Riggs to construct needed buildings.[55] Riggs's appointment of Lee, which marked the beginning of a campus building style that reflected Lee's propensity for the Italian landscape and climate, lasted more than thirty years.

RUDOLPH E. LEE

Students and visitors remember the Clemson campus for the distinctive buildings of multi-colored brick and terra cotta roofs, details of the Italian Renaissance style that Rudolph Lee loved and incorporated into his many campus buildings. Lee reinterpreted the Collegiate Gothic designs of Bruce and Morgan, designers of the original buildings, and for more than three decades Lee's vision dominated the design of campus buildings.

A native of Anderson, South Carolina, Lee received his undergraduate education at Clemson College and graduated in the class of 1896. As college architect, Lee received a commission to design the YMCA Building, later named Holtzendorff Hall, which was the first "student life" building on campus. Other buildings followed: Sikes Hall library renovation (1924), Riggs Hall (1927), Field House (1927), Barracks quadrangle (1935–36), Long Hall (1937), Sirrine Hall (1938) and Norris Hall (1938).

Lee did not confine himself to work at Clemson, however. He led a statewide campaign for better school buildings and school safety, and designed buildings in the town of Clemson. Near the end of his tenure at Clemson, Lee's interests turned toward preserving historical structures when the Hanover House was relocated to the Clemson campus. His plans to situate the structure in a suitable context, which he called "Colonial Farm Life Restoration," intrigued Boston architects Perry, Shaw and Hepburn, Kehoe and Dean, but never came to fruition. Lee's work led to the formation of the Clemson Architectural Foundation in 1940; to recognize his many contributions the architecture building was named Lee Hall in 1966.

18

SB 1–2 Lee, circa 1911

In construction, the Riggs years witnessed successes in erecting a horticulture barn, barracks, and his pride and joy, Holtzendorff Hall.[56] Yet other seemingly innocuous projects, such as "a little toilet pavilion," which Riggs wanted "for the convenience of picnickers visiting the campus," proved impossible to fund and went unbuilt.[57] The two-story pavilion, planned for a site near the Dairy Building (now the parking lot behind Sikes Hall), would have featured a lower story "equipped for public comfort" and an upper story "of open construction suitable for open air concerts and performances which will be viewed by spectators seated on the surrounding hillsides and looking across a small lake that will lie between the hills and the pavilion."[58] Other repeated requests for a laundry and hospital, which he called "pressing needs," went unmet.[59]

Repeated rejections prompted Riggs to formulate a new method of prioritizing building requests, using lists of building needs that were submitted to the Executive Committee of the Trustees. After approval, the lists became part of the overall budget request submitted to the state. However, on at least one occasion Riggs made his request in person before Governor Robert A. Cooper, who had asked for higher education building programs covering ten years, a period Riggs had advocated since he assumed the presidency. By 1920, however, Riggs took a more realistic, or perhaps jaded, view; he wrote at the top of that year's list of seventeen needed buildings that "with our resources, it is impossible to erect a single one."[60] College operations in his time depended upon the revenues obtained from the state tax on fertilizers; those revenues, in turn, were dependent upon the vagaries of climate, a favorable growing season, and the support of the state legislature—a body Riggs believed should "support and develop" Clemson "by every consideration of patriotism and self-interest," but which for various reasons did not. To the Trustees he expressed hope that the legislature would eventually find a way to finance building construction "more logical than an addition for buildings to the current budget."[61] In his prescient "Ten Year Building Program," submitted in 1923, Riggs thoughtfully laid out Clemson's needs: dormitories, a hospital, a laundry, a community store, and better faculty housing. That request also proved his last; he died unexpectedly in 1924.

Campus development in the years that followed faced adversity. Yet, in spite of the hard times, more than a dozen buildings were constructed; only two went unbuilt. South Carolina prohibited state institutions from using fees or other funds for the erection of buildings[62] and a sluggish state economy, which signaled the onset of the Great Depression, militated against the building construction regardless of purpose.[63] But the depressed economy also presented an opportunity that new President Sikes seized. Seemingly undaunted by the dismal economy but cognizant of South Carolina's burgeoning textile industry, Sikes championed a textile education building, rather than a new agricultural building, as his top priority. Other buildings on his list included an infirmary, a new mechanical engineering building to replace the one destroyed by fire in 1926, and a building for "physical education," which Sikes separated from athletics. He ultimately succeeded in getting two of the four. Because of "growing sentiment in the legislature against appropriating money for buildings" some counseled Sikes to divert money from the operating budget for building projects, but he refused, saying that to do so jeopardized the teaching work of the college.[64] He proposed instead to negotiate directly with Washington DC for federal funds from the Works Project Administration (WPA), rather than work through the State Planning Board. His strategy worked. The WPA, Sikes, Lee, and business manager J. C. Littlejohn teamed up seven times in the 1930s to produce new buildings.[65] These included five dormitories, the Agricultural Hall, and the Textile Building.[66] Sikes's efforts in the 1930s also procured the acreage that later became the Clemson Experimental Forest.[67]

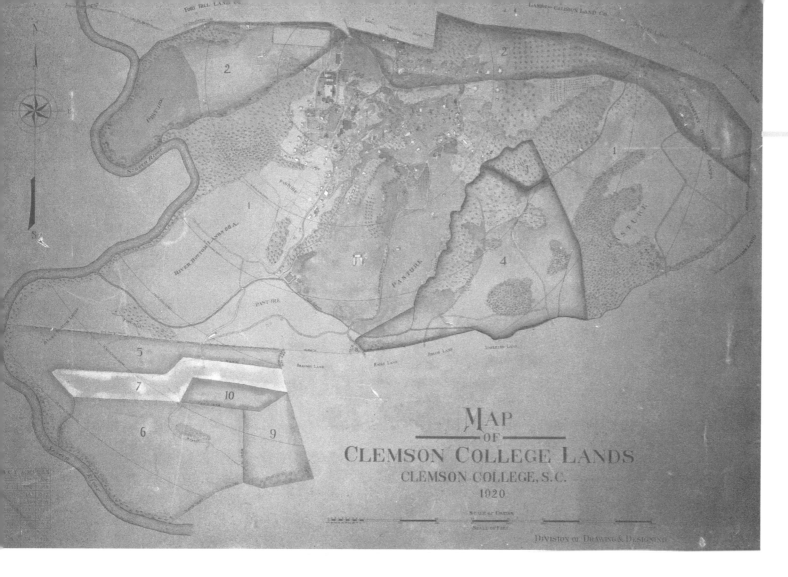

The outstanding record of building accomplishments and miniscule number of unbuilt projects stand as the major contribution of the Sikes years in campus development. Even more significant than his record, however, was his approach to development: determining the locations of dormitories, the hospital, and roads without the use of topographical studies or detailed campus maps, but with only the assistance of a "building committee," about which he provided few details.[68] Sikes, assisted by Littlejohn, astutely analyzed information and statistics, projected enrollments, student demographics, sources of income, teaching activities, and the financing of buildings; their work prefigured modern campus planning methodology by at least a decade.[69] Sikes demonstrated that diligence, thought, and creativity could overcome INCREDIBLY ADVERSE ECONOMIC CONDITIONS.[70]

Sikes's successor, Robert F. Poole, the first alumnus to serve as president of Clemson, took office in July 1940. Poole's academic background as a plant pathologist and his resume of activities in professional associations matched the economic needs of South Carolina and Clemson College, but it did not include expertise or experience in campus planning.[71] To assist him in this sphere of his duties, Poole created the Buildings and Grounds Committee, an expanded version of the building committee used by his predecessor. This group, which consisted of both professional staff and faculty members, charted the course for campus development for the next ten years, but their influence was felt for decades beyond. Its scope of authority ran the gamut of activities associated with campus planning and development: recommending building sites, removing buildings, locating and naming roads and buildings, numbering houses, signage, land purchases, property development, and timber cutting.[72] Throughout the 1940s the Buildings and Grounds Committee furnished Poole with figures on construction costs, enrollment, and other areas of concern. These were addressed by college deans whose feedback Poole included, along with committee recommendations, in his reports to the Trustees.[73]

The entry of the United States into World War II in December 1941 interrupted any plans Poole might have had for campus development. With that global conflagration life at Clemson, as most experienced it, drastically changed. At least half of the students left for military service, and would return home after the war. Poole oversaw Clemson during these tumultuous years, which marked its transition into a modern institution. His nostalgic and agrarian view of Clemson, based in part on his own memories of student life, help to explain his approach to campus development. The unbuilt projects of Poole's administration invited nostalgia, and were often peculiar to an earlier period or style, reflecting a preoccupation with bygone days. These projects, due to their merits and the perseverance of their sponsors, were the subject of years of repeated discussion and debate. With the exception of the arboretum, which reprised an earlier effort, ALL OF THESE PROJECTS WERE BUILDINGS.

THE ESTABLISHMENT OF AN arboretum, while not strictly an architectural project, held ramifications for campus development and building construction. Had the original plans been followed on the lands proposed, a nature reserve would have impacted the sites of buildings, placement of roads, and locations of other services for years to come. "Arboreta," meaning plots of land on which many different trees or shrubs are grown for study and display, had a long heritage in Europe, but were relatively new to the United States. Here they began as gardens planted by affluent families (or their hired landscape architects) on large estates or plantations which were later ceded to state governments and academic institutions, especially those with agricultural and scientific missions.[74] As mentioned above, planning for an arboretum at Clemson originated with President Mell's attempt to hire Kelsey to improve the campus grounds.

ARBORETUM

1941–1948

Mell had developed an arboretum at the State College in Alabama (now Auburn University) before coming to South Carolina and wanted to create something similar at Clemson: "This has been under way [sic] at Clemson College ever since I have been connected with the institution, and it has been my endeavor to establish within the grounds some 200 acres, all the trees and shrubs of interest in our native forests."[75] Kelsey, encouraged by Mell's interest, expressed his pleasure that an agricultural college planned to develop a scientific arboretum:[76]

> It is one of my sincerest hopes that the South will have an adequate arboretum which contains all of the native flora of a shrubby nature that can be grown there and possibly exotics. I know of none outside of St. Louis and south of the Mason and Dixon Line.[77]

Without an agreement between Kelsey and the Trustees over his fees, however, plans for an arboretum halted.

Soon after Poole became president, however, he recommended to the Trustees that the site "surrounding the old spring near the field house and the proposed stadium [Memorial Stadium], be set aside as a Naturalist Park [sic],"[78] a phrase which was not defined in the extant records. The Trustees agreed with Poole and approved his recommendation, yet took no further action—perhaps because they were aware that others were interested in developing a larger area.[79] Later in the year, the Buildings and Grounds committee passed a formal resolution recommending that all the woodland on campus and College lands be considered an arboretum and proposed a ban on cutting timber, except for that which was dead or necessary for construction.[80] Discussions resumed in 1944 when Chemistry Professor C. C. Newman proposed to the Buildings and Grounds Committee "that the whole College property be treated as an arboretum."[81] The Committee responded to Newman's proposal by convening a subcommittee to study the issue and make recommendations, but again took no further action. Four years later, the Buildings and Grounds Committee again took up the idea, this time commending efforts to label trees and shrubs on many parts of the College property. Now they specified an area "between the Stadium, Water street [sic], and the physical education plant" (the same area Poole had wanted for a naturalist park), and formally asked the administration to officially designate it as an arboretum. An arboretum, the committee found, "would have to be developed over a long period of years, particularly at an institution where there is no special fund for such a purpose."[82]

In October 1948 the Buildings and Grounds Committee submitted a "Tentative Proposal" to create an arboretum. It called for setting aside eighty-two acres consisting of sixty woodland acres east of the Sheep Barn, south of Highway 76; twenty acres in the Stadium/Cemetery Hill [now Woodland Cemetery] area; and two acres bounded by Water Street, the Stadium, Field House, and the C&R [Construction and Repair] Shop. This plan proposed the "Kress Arboretum," which would be funded by a bequest from C. W. Kress and the Kress Foundation because of Kress's interest in floriculture.[83] But because the proposal was received too late for the Trustees' upcoming October meeting, they did not consider the issue and the minutes recorded no further action on the proposal.[84] Although the arboretum project continued to receive support from advocates who urged the college administration to "keep the area intact and sacred to this purpose,"[85] their efforts foundered for another decade. Eventually the arboretum became reality as part of a botanical garden on the sixty-acre site east of the Sheep Barn. That location, rather than the two proposed earlier for the campus proper, freed space for the construction projects that followed.

In addition to the arboretum, three more unbuilt projects demonstrated Poole's view of campus development and building projects: the Clemson Little Theater (May 1941); the Colonial Restoration Area (August 1941); and the Colonial Farm Life Restoration (1945). Each project fit the provincial, "backward glance" mode of thinking, and reside within the contingent category of unbuilt architecture. Two of the projects originated with architect Rudolph Lee and one with the Class of 1916; EACH EXHIBITED A UNIQUE VISION OF CLEMSON.

UNBUILT PROJECTS DURING THE POOLE ADMINISTRATION

THE CLEMSON LITTLE THEATER (MAY 1941)

THE COLONIAL RESTORATION AREA (AUGUST 1941)

THE COLONIAL FARM LIFE RESTORATION (1945)

From the first years of Clemson's existence, dramatic performances and plays contributed significantly to college life. Students, faculty, and staff belonged to various groups with a focus on the dramatic arts. By the 1930s cadets had formed clubs, such as the Clemson College Drama Circle and Clemson Community Players, to produce plays and dramatic performances. Venues for these productions included the college chapel in the Main Building and the Clemson Calhoun School, located off campus. Other events such as concerts were held at the Outdoor Theater and the Field House. Since no on-campus venue had adequate seating for performances, in 1941 the Class of 1916 undertook a campaign to erect a theater building.

CLEMSON LITTLE THEATER
MAY 1941

FIG. 1-10
Clemson Little Theater in Conception

CLEMSON COLLEGE LITTLE THEATER BY CLASS 1916

Their plan for the Clemson Little Theater (there would be later versions), appeared in the student newspaper, *The Tiger*, on May 17, 1941—the same issue published a rendering of the new Memorial Stadium on the front page. Headlined "Clemson Little Theater by Class 1916," the article included an architect's drawing of the new building. An executive committee, headed by Class President R. Brice Waters and whose membership included President Poole, drew up the plans. The building was to be of brick construction, and plans specified a "spacious stage" for plays, an orchestra, and debate practice, for use "in all types of weather."[86] In an effort to cut costs the plans specified that the Little Theater be constructed on the foundation of the college print shop (near present-day Olin Hall). The 109 members of the Class of 1916 set their contribution at $10,000 for the building project,[87] while the remaining construction costs were covered by an existing appropriation from the WPA for general campus improvements. The cornerstone, to be laid at the twenty-fifth reunion of the class during graduation on May 31, 1941, failed to occur for unspecified reasons, most likely due to the imminent threat of America's entrance into World War II. Despite the best efforts of the Class of 1916, the campaign to secure a home for the Little Theater struggled on for more than a decade.

CLEMSON LITTLE THEATRE BUILDING J.H. GATES ARCHITECT

FIG. 1-11 *Clemson Little Theater in Sheep Barn*

In June 1951 the Class of 1916 enlisted the assistance of the Department of Architecture to convert the Sheep Barn, built in 1903 on the east side of campus, for the Little Theater. President Poole approved the recommendation of Architecture Professor John Gates and the department to convert the barn using faculty and student workers, and the Trustees approved the plans.[88] Gates presented his sketches, which he called "the Sheep Barn Playhouse" in the drawings, at the meeting of the Buildings and Grounds Committee in July 1951. However, the plans he presented combined the Little Theater with a college museum in the barn. Gates also presented a plot plan, prepared years earlier by Lee, of other buildings for possible construction in the area called "Colonial Circle," adjacent to the barn and home to Hanover House. The Buildings and Grounds Committee approved the "general idea" of Gates's plans, but they did not approve using the Sheep Barn as a combined theater and museum "due to the 'inflammable nature'" of the building,[89] even though *The Tiger* reported in October 1951 that the renovation was getting underway.[90]

When architects Perry, Shaw and Hepburn, Kehoe and Dean (PSHKD) produced the campus master plan in 1953, Thomas Shaw proposed, and the Trustees approved, a new location for the Little Theater,[91] projected on the plan as "Future Theater," just east of the library.[92] After waiting for another two years, with no building forthcoming, the Class of 1916 contacted Head of the Department of Architecture Harlan E. McClure in April 1956 to develop new plans for the theater between the small and large gymnasia. McClure wrote Poole that the location had "much to recommend it since mechanical services were already available and three of the existing walls could be used in their present state."[93] The Trustees, however, did not agree when they met that same month.[94] With that setback, the staff of the Little Theater moved performances to the auditorium in the Food Industries Building,[95] where they remained until THE THEATER MOVED OFF CAMPUS.

29

THE RELOCATION OF A historic structure to the campus precipitated a series of events that resulted in unrealized visions and two unbuilt projects. Hanover House, constructed by Paul De St. Julien in Berkeley County circa 1714–16, faced inundation by the construction of Lake Moultrie, a project of Santee-Cooper.[96] The house had been offered to a museum and several organizations in the low country, but all declined. Clemson, the only school in South Carolina with an architecture department, enjoyed close ties to the Ravenel family, one of the earliest families to own and occupy the old house.[97] After Trustee Robert M. Cooper and architect Lee recommended saving the house by bringing it to campus,[98] the newly constituted Buildings and Grounds Committee determined a location on which to reassemble it. Committee members David Watson, superintendent of grounds, and Littlejohn, the business manager, recommended a knoll adjacent to the Sheep Barn on the east side of campus. Professor H. E. Glenn mapped the area, but also indicated other "possible locations for historic houses which may be in the future acquired by Clemson." The Building and Grounds Committee further called for developing "in the area a suitable garden and in keeping with the time in which the structure was built," and creating access to the area with access via a new street named "Colonial Drive [sic]."[99]

COLONIAL RESTORATION AREA

AUGUST 1941

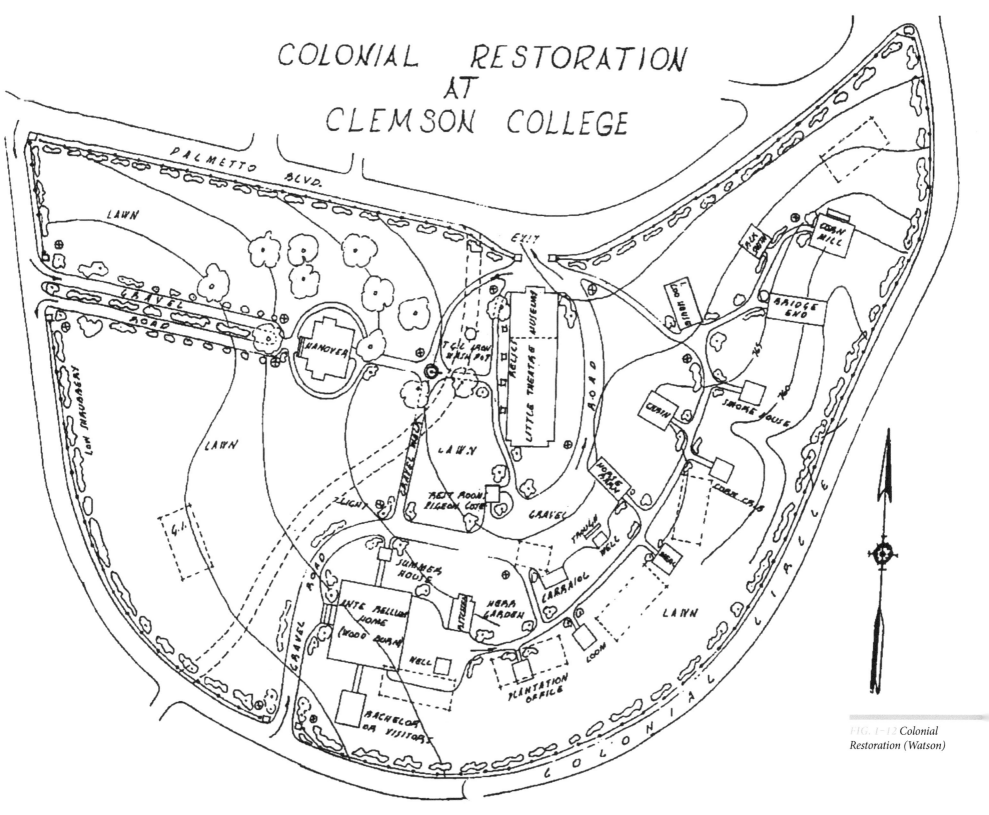

FIG. 1-12 Colonial Restoration (Watson)

The report of the Buildings and Grounds Committee, written by Watson and forwarded to President Poole by Littlejohn, provided additional details about the committee's discussion:

> The question arose about the number of historic residences that might be moved to the campus. Due consideration was given to this possibility and feeling that in time there might be other houses of like kind brought to the campus, the committee thought of the possibility of putting these houses on the ridge leading out behind the sheep barn toward Mr. Ted Cook's residence. In other words, a street might be built leading …around the knoll back to the road…and these historic houses be built facing this street…In case there are to be no other residences built on the campus, the whole east side of Palmetto Boulevard might be given over to these historic houses. Should there be others, it [the committee] recommends the space immediately north of the sheep barn.[100]

Acting on Littlejohn's recommendation, Poole reported to the Trustees in October 1941 the proposal to name the street "Colonial *Circle*" (author's emphasis), a slight deviation from the name the committee suggested, and to add buildings there.[101] It was not until June 1946 that the Trustees approved the new road under that name.[102] Lee prepared a plot plan for this "restoration area," as it came to be known, which showed the locations where old structures could be erected and restored.[103]

President Poole approved the Committee's recommendation and in August 1941 the painstaking removal of Hanover House commenced. This was followed by a two-year reassembly process, which did not occur until after the end of the war. Just after completing the reassembly, Watson wrote President Poole asking for funds to erect two log houses in the area; Poole expressed no interest but held the request for approval by the Trustees.[104] The issue surfaced again over a decade later when the Buildings and Grounds Committee met to discuss adding historic structures to the area; the Committee convened specifically to discuss relocating an old log house, which was once used as a residence, to the restoration area. Some members of the committee wanted the 18' x 32' house to be located on the east side of the barn, as Lee had drawn in the original plot plan, while other members preferred the west side, where the newly reassembled Hanover House now stood.[105] President Poole resolved the matter in a handwritten reply at the bottom of the letter Watson had written asking for approval: "Mr. Shaw [architect with PSHKD] expects to be here soon. Let him take a look at the log house. He may have some good suggestions."[106] After further study of the issue, Shaw and the architects recommended placing the log house on the east side of the Sheep Barn as Lee had first proposed, and in January 1955 it was reconstructed there.[107] But, in spite of the cabin's fortuitous reconstruction and the continuing efforts of Watson and alumni, the Colonial Restoration Area never fully developed; Hanover House and Hunt Cabin were the only structures moved there. When campus growth encroached and the two structures became impediments to progress,[108] they were relocated to the South Carolina Botanical Garden—THE HUNT CABIN IN 1979 AND HANOVER HOUSE IN 1994.

ONE OF LEE'S PROPOSALS, the creation of a "Colonial Farm Life Restoration Area" in 1945, exemplified the provincial mindset. It differed from Watson's earlier plan, in which Lee had assisted, to create a historic district near the Sheep Barn. Lee, who had designed numerous buildings for colleges and schools in South Carolina and was responsible for nearly the entire Clemson campus circa 1945, turned his attention to the creation of an historic district within a college campus—an unusual idea at the time that was later adopted by many colleges and universities which owned historic properties.[109] The location Lee identified for the restoration, underutilized acreage at the rear of Fort Hill (now the site of Lee and Lowry Halls and the Fluor-Daniel Building), was the site of "old mule barns" and several other structures targeted for removal.[110] At that time, the location afforded an unobstructed view of the rear of the adjoining Fort Hill property.

33

Since his papers and other University sources provide no clues, one can only speculate as to Lee's reasons for choosing this location. Perhaps he intended to contrast small-scale farm life with the plantation life typified by Fort Hill. Or perhaps he desired a new building for the study of architecture, which had grown in importance since becoming part of the curriculum, and believed juxtaposing this new building with a historical village would increase the likelihood of achieving both objectives. Whatever his thinking, Lee first presented his plans to the members of the Buildings and Grounds Committee in March. His village consisted of three main elements: a formal entrance at which he positioned the "future architecture building;" a "front court," immediately behind, which showcased a structure Lee labeled as an "antebellum house,"[111] with a sweeping front lawn and several smaller houses alongside driveways lined with rail fencing; and a "rear court," which contained Watson's log cabin, a corn crib, grist mill, pigeon house, gourd houses for purple martins, a weave room, the overseer's kitchen at Fort Hill, and several other quarters for field hands. The setting was complemented by landscaping consisting of magnolia, crepe myrtle, boxwood, holly, and native flowering plants. The presentation impressed the Buildings and Grounds Committee, which responded favorably but "decided to defer action" until a campus map, in production by Professor Glenn and alumnus F. R. Sweeny, was completed and several roads laid out. "We thought the restoration a fine idea," Watson stated, "but preferred not to take definite action on it at this time."[112] President Poole, similarly, expressed hesitancy to Watson a few days later:

> I am sure that your Committee is interested in suggestions and proposals from any of your members or from any groups on the campus, but I think we should consider most carefully all the proposals before any special project is undertaken. I am thinking in particular of the restoration project referred to in the minutes.[113]

Poole never expressly stated in writing the reasons for his hesitation, but viewed Lee's plans, and any support he would give the project, as not in accord with the thinking of the Trustees.[114]

Lee's Colonial Farm Life Restoration effort followed another of his proposals, which had debuted in April 1945. In its March 2 issue *The Tiger* published a graphic of Lee's "New Chemistry Building" front and center on page one. This was a typical Lee design that featured an Italianate three-story building with two towers, each five stories high. Its construction, estimated at $600,000, would have met the needs of the 3,500 to 4,000 students expected to attend Clemson after the war.[115] When fire destroyed much of the Chemistry Building in August 1946, the timing seemed to guarantee the construction of Lee's new design. Instead, the Trustees decided to restore the burned structure without a pitched roof, rather than construct a new building. Lee's reaction to the decision not to pursue his design for the Chemistry Building and to delay his Colonial Farm Life Restoration project remain unknown; he retired as college architect in 1948. But he may have derived a degree of satisfaction when in 1953 the Buildings and Grounds Committee recommended the submission of his Colonial Farm Life Restoration plans to architects PSHKD (the firm hired to complete a campus master plan in 1952) for review and approval.[116] Although the Boston architects did not set aside space for Lee's project, they designated an area called "Future Engineering Group" in a layout that bore a striking resemblance to part of Lee's Colonial Farm Life Restoration; the architecture building, originally positioned at the entrance of Lee's project, was shifted a hundred feet to the west of the site Lee originally proposed.[117]

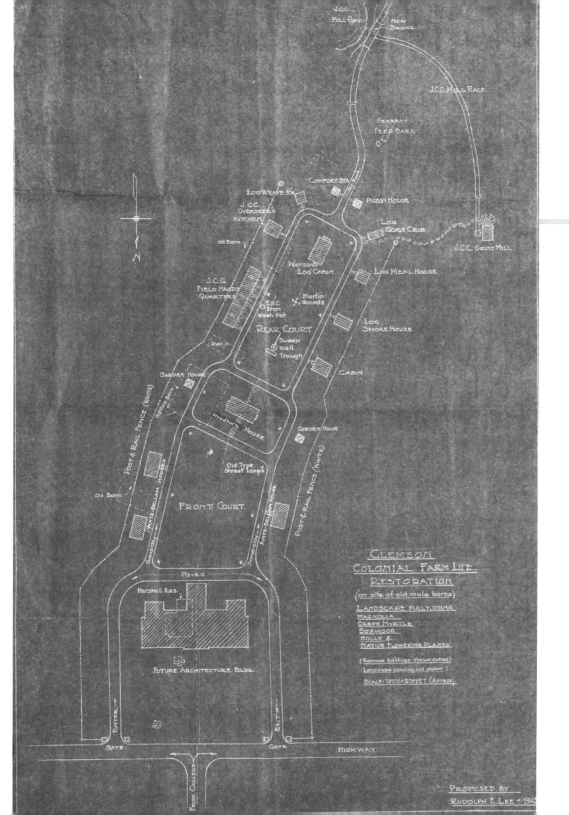

FIG. 1-13

Colonial Farm Life
(Lee Plan) 1945

35

At face value the Lee designs, as well as the other unbuilt projects of the Poole era, represented a particular genre that never caught on. Without doubt the projects closed a chapter of campus planning and development that was out of step with the tenor of the times, which embraced fresh starts and new beginnings. The nostalgic visions of the Poole-era projects marked the end of Lee's style of campus architecture, in effect since 1911, and the beginning of a new era in campus planning and development, in both theory and practice. The red-orange brick, bracketed eaves, red tile roofs, and Romanesque motifs—elements of the style which characterized all of Lee's buildings—also unified the campus aesthetically; soon a new style would perform a similar function. The changes signaled more than a shift in style: they marked the end of an approach to campus planning based on expediency and immediate needs and the beginning of one characterized by a view toward the future. In practical terms, the unbuilt projects meant that there would be no living history village, no building exclusively for the study of architecture (at least for another decade), and no theater building for another forty years. The decision not to construct these projects belied an unspoken view of campus planning and historic preservation that confined historic structures to specific areas—the grounds of Fort Hill and near the Sheep Barn. Not until the 1990s did a more fully articulated view of historic preservation become an integral part of master planning.

Lee's departure coincided with other momentous changes in the postwar years. In 1944 President Poole received data from Business Manager Littlejohn that 2,500–3,000 men would return to Clemson seeking to complete their education, with possibly 5,000–7,000 others hoping to attend a few years after the war ended; he estimated $3 million would be needed for a building program.

In preparation for the influx Poole instructed the Buildings and Grounds Committee to "get a number of roads laid out by the highway department as to provide for buildings" and to study these sites for proposed new buildings, to be erected following the end of the year.[118] He also suggested that civil engineering students could help plan the new roads and that students studying architecture aid in drawing building plans.[119]

Littlejohn and the Building and Grounds Committee prioritized the need for new buildings as follows: first, chemistry, followed by a boiler plant, barracks, and a hospital.[120] Poole sent the findings to the Trustees in June 1945 with the title "Post-War Educational Plans" with the cryptic remark that "we are dipping far into the future."[121] He cogently made the case for "more and better faculty, buildings, and equipment," to remain a "progressive institution."[122] The Trustees authorized a $6 million post-war building program[123]—an action that anticipated the predicted postwar growth, but not all of the problems that it created. A new phenomenon, traffic congestion, took center stage. "Large numbers of veterans have brought cars to Clemson," Poole wrote the Trustees, "and, thus far, a satisfactory plan has not been developed."[124] That admission signaled the beginning of a long-term problem, as the automobile became the principal factor in postwar campus planning, not just at Clemson, but at campuses nationwide.[125] Veterans drove to campus and needed space to park their cars and "noisy motorcycles"—which they did, alongside roads or in rapidly constructed lots, as well as lots which had not been prepared.[126] The automobile, and its associated parking issues, heralded a new aspect of campus planning and building construction that challenged campus planners and administrators ever since.

NEW CHEMISTRY BUILDING

FIG. 1-14 Lee Chemistry Building

CLEMSON COLLEGE CHEMISTRY BUILDING

Growing enrollment also forced college officials to think in non-traditional ways and to plan quickly to accommodate students—for example, using the hospital annex for classroom space, scheduling classes at night, creating larger classes, repurposing the gym and upper floor of Godfrey Hall for sleeping quarters, and providing living quarters to married veterans (one of the few institutions in the nation to do so).[127] To remedy the housing problem, Littlejohn worked with US Senator Burnet Maybank and John H. Gates of the Federal Housing Administration to create emergency housing for veterans which consisted of fifty-seven duplex apartments, 248 single unit houses, and three temporary barracks. The duplexes and houses, which were also called "UK homes" because they were manufactured in the United Kingdom, were clustered in two "colonies"—one on the south campus where President Poole hoped to build an agricultural

complex, and the other near present-day Memorial Stadium.[128] The federal government paid the cost of demounting, moving, and rebuilding the units.[129]

The unparalleled growth in enrollment and the need for new buildings brought changes to functions and operations that had served for decades. The diligent efforts of college presidents to develop the campus had sometimes succeeded, but had just as often failed because of the vagaries of financing, conflicting agendas, or competing priorities. The pendulum of campus planning and construction—heretofore the exclusive domain of the Trustees and the President—now swung to THE DEPARTMENT OF ARCHITECTURE.

37

CHAPTER TWO

"CASUALTIES" OF MODERNIZATION

1947–1989

FIG. 2-1 *Clemson House lobby, 1950*

THE UNPRECEDENTED AND SUSTAINED growth in enrollment after World War II produced a new order at Clemson. Enrollment, which stood at 2,300 students in 1940, grew to just over 4,000 by 1960, and a record-setting 10,891 by 1980.[1] This growth engendered traffic congestion, a variety of athletic events that attracted large audiences, and an expanding curriculum for burgeoning fields of study; all required new and sophisticated approaches to planning. Campus planning efforts, which had heretofore focused on traditional styles and piecemeal solutions, gave way to comprehensive planning that embraced a formalized, systematized view of development concerned with growth and change. The new approach also embraced an aggressive and expensive construction agenda that ultimately yielded an up-to-date campus with an array of modern buildings, but also led to some design casualties.

The move toward modernization began in 1947, when John H. "Rusty" Gates became the new head of the Department of Architecture and assumed leadership in campus planning. Gates, a Yale-trained architect and former housing officer for the Federal Housing Authority, had come to Clemson to develop ways to house veterans and faculty. His April 1948 study on housing recommended several solutions, among them, an apartment house to accommodate visitors and short-term faculty. The new structure, the Clemson House Hotel, designed in the International Style, marked a dramatic departure from his predecessor Lee's buildings, in that it emphasized bands of brick and masonry punctuated with areas of glass and little, if any, ornamentation. Constructed by Charles Daniel in 1950 and used until its demolition in December 2017, Clemson House was the first of Daniel's numerous modern campus buildings, constructed over a period of more than twenty years.

FIG. 2-2 *PSHKD*
Master Plan

Aside from housing solutions, Gates and Professor Gilmer "Pete" Petroff, also a Yale-trained architect, began work in July 1948 on a map of the campus that indicated the sites of future buildings. The map, which was formed by piecing together sections of a topographical map created by members of the Civil Engineering department in 1945, was called at the time Clemson's first campus master plan, and rightly so.[2] It showed the proposed expansion of the College through a long-range building program, with buildings numbered in order of construction priority (the hospital being first). The map designated the proposed building locations using colors to differentiate areas of the campus and groups of buildings. For future building construction, Gates recommended the use of red brick with limestone trim, a marked departure from Lee's Italianate style with its multi-colored brick. Gates and Petroff completed the plan in time for President Robert Franklin Poole to present it to the Trustees in October 1948. Pleased with the result, the Trustees approved and President Poole proudly hung the master plan in his office.[3]

In the process of producing their plan, Gates and Petroff brought to the forefront issues of campus development that demanded immediate attention: insufficient study space, lack of parking, and, most urgent, the imminent inundation of college lands by the reservoir to be formed by the construction of Hartwell Dam.[4] Two committees, convened by President Poole to study the effects of the dam, concluded that the projected backwater would flood 615 acres of bottomlands, Memorial Stadium, the water disposal plant, thirty-five prefab units, all housing west of the stadium, hay barns, several power lines, and roads—all of which would cripple campus growth and expansion.[5] Those committee findings, and discussions with the Army Corps of Engineers on ways to prevent the loss of lands, clearly pointed to the need for professional expertise in campus planning and a long range development plan.[6] In 1952 the Trustees authorized Business Manager J. C. Littlejohn to "seek out suitable architects to create a long range master plan."[7] Littlejohn discovered that nearby Furman University in Greenville had employed the firm of Perry, Shaw and Hepburn, Kehoe and Dean (PSHKD) of Boston to design its new campus. Upon contacting the architects, Littlejohn was informed that if the Clemson Trustees hired the firm, the cost would be cut by half for each institution.[8]

"The Master Plan," as it was called in promotional material from 1954, embodied the latest concepts in campus planning.[9] It established zones for administration, academics, housing, and student activities, all accommodated in a military-style layout featuring quadrangles and straight lines, in keeping with Clemson's military tradition. The plan projected a total of eighteen new buildings. In the short term, the master plan set the stage for construction of modern buildings: Barnett, Benet, Cope, Geer, Johnstone, Lever, Manning, Martin, Mauldin, Sanders, and Young halls, for housing; in academics, the engineering complex (Lee and Lowry halls), agricultural complex (the Plant and Animal Science Building and Newman Hall), physics building (Kinard Hall), Robert Muldrow Cooper Library, Daniel Hall, and Strode Tower; and in student activities, Redfern Health Center and Schilletter and Harcombe dining halls. Over the long term, the master plan laid the foundation for better planning and management of resources, and provided the skeleton for campus development for the next three decades.[10]

Master Plan

1. Administration Building
2. Chapel
3. Future Y.M.C.A. Addition
4. Y.M.C.A.
5. Post Office
6. Barracks
7. Future Barracks
8. Laundry
9. Service Division
11. Memorial Stadium
12. Auditorium and Coliseum

13. Waterworks
14. Future Armory
15. Calhoun Mansion
16. Future Classroom Building
17. Amphitheater
18. Chemistry Building
19. Present Library
20. Clemson House Hotel
21. Housing
22. Future Theater
23. Future Physics Building

24. Agriculture Building
25. Future Women's Dormitory
27. Future Women's Dining Hall
28. Future Classroom Building
29. Future Classroom Building
30. Future Library
31. Ceramics Building
32. Engineering Building
33. Future Addition to Student Shops
34. Student Shops
35. Textile Building

36. Future Textile Building
37. Future Textile Building
38. Future Infirmary
39. Future Architecture Building
40. Future Agricultural Building
44. Dairy Laboratory
45. Dairy Barn
46. New Agriculture Group
47. Future Agriculture Buildings
48. Future Engineering Group
49. New Dining Hall

PERRY, SHAW AND HEPBURN, KEHOE AND DEAN

John D. Rockefeller, Jr. retained Boston architect William Graves Perry to restore historic Williamsburg, VA, a project that lasted ten years and launched the reputation of Perry and his firm as planners of academic campuses. Joined by architects Thomas Mott Shaw, Andrew Hopewell Hepburn, Christopher M. Kehoe and Robert Charles Dean, the Boston firm specialized in colonial revival, a style that matched the needs and desires of numerous academic institutions in laying out their campuses.

Clemson College leaders, however, wanted a different style, and those views resonated with Dean, a skilled draftsman and retired brigadier general, who was grounded in Georgian architecture, but who, according to his partners, "was anxious to cut his teeth on modern." The campus master plan produced by the firm for Clemson consisted of a generalized map, bird's-eye perspective, and projections for twenty-nine new buildings, among them an agricultural complex, textile building, and dormitories. It placed a new library at the center of campus, in accord with the philosophy of educational practice held by architect Perry, who believed that students needed time for private reflection and study apart from communal living. The plan also heralded Clemson's coeducational future— though there were no stated plans to make Clemson

SB 2-1 Architects Perry, Shaw, and Hepburn

College coeducational in 1953—by projecting a future dormitory and a dining hall for women. In what would later be called "zones" or "precincts," the plan created specific areas for housing, dining, and academics that reflected a regimented and orderly military style befitting a military college.

Years after its creation in 1953, the plan continued to receive acknowledgments from campus planners on its soundness and vision. It marked a milestone in campus development.

The master plan changed the focus of campus development by shifting the center of campus, heretofore concentrated around Fort Hill, eastward.[11] That shift may be observed in the working papers produced by architects as they analyzed the data collected and proposed schemes, as prelude to the final report, to deal with Clemson's growth and topography. One scheme prominently embraced green space: it suggested a botanical garden, encircled by numerous academic buildings, just north of the Outdoor Theater,[12] and an "academic center" to the south that featured a "library garden" and a new library, surrounded by buildings housing architecture, education, and agriculture.[13] Another scheme, one that raised concern for Clemson officials, placed a group of interconnected agricultural buildings behind and slightly east of Long Hall. These included separate buildings for extension, agronomy, botany, horticulture, food technology, dairy, animal husbandry, and poultry. A revised scheme, revealed in 1953, removed the botanical garden, theater, and museum from the academic area and relocated the agricultural buildings from the Long Hall area to one on the horticulture grounds. After Clemson officials reviewed the plan and objected, the architects countered with a proposal which moved the location of the agricultural buildings to the west (the current location of Poole and Newman halls) and changed the size, shape, and arrangement of the buildings to their current form.[14] Clemson agreed to these changes and the South Carolina State Highway Department began immediate surveys for road and street changes, among the first a road on the campus perimeter, now Silas Pearman Boulevard.[15]

Shifting the focus of development eastward, however, created challenges for some of the new building sites that the architects wanted, but Clemson opposed. Architect Thomas Shaw believed that the new physics building (now Kinard Hall) was well placed, but that the new classroom building (Daniel Hall) was not "happily related" to the physics building or to Long Hall; he wanted to align the west wing of the classroom building with the west elevation of the physics building to form a quadrangle for a new library.[16] Professor H. E. "Pop" Glenn, speaking for Clemson, pointed out that to do so would cause the library to stand directly over a ravine 30 feet deep and 70 feet wide.[17] Glenn also opposed the proposed location for the projected structural sciences building, as it would be inundated by the waters of the Hartwell reservoir.[18] Exchanges between the two continued until the architects acceded to the changes Clemson wanted. Faults aside, though, the master plan succeeded admirably. It placed buildings symmetrically along an axis,[19] and depicted future buildings in a modern style. Although the plan employed the convention of campus planning at the time to predetermine the position and forms of buildings, it adopted an approach that emphasized future growth and architectural variety, considered desirable characteristics by most campus planners.[20]

Although the master plan set the course for modern campus planning, other events helped stay it. In 1955 the Trustees hired management consultants Cresap, McCormick and Paget (CMP) of New York to conduct an extensive review of the college's organization. Their product, although not technically a campus master plan, nevertheless served in a de facto capacity, working in tandem with the 1953 master plan. The CMP report, published in four volumes, confronted Clemson's planning issues without equivocation: "No one person in the present organization [sic] structure has the assigned responsibility for planning the college's future."[21] For that reason, the consultants recommended a "Vice-president for Development" to coordinate all plans affecting the future of the College: the College master plan, the development of units within the plan, building priorities, construction standards, and the means of developing outside capital to finance development.[22] To implement the changes prescribed, the Trustees hired textile executive R. C. Edwards as Vice-president for Development in 1958. His appointment and subsequent election as President after the death of President Poole, along with the contemporaneous appointment of Harlan McClure as head of the School of Architecture, guaranteed the changes the Trustees desired.[23]

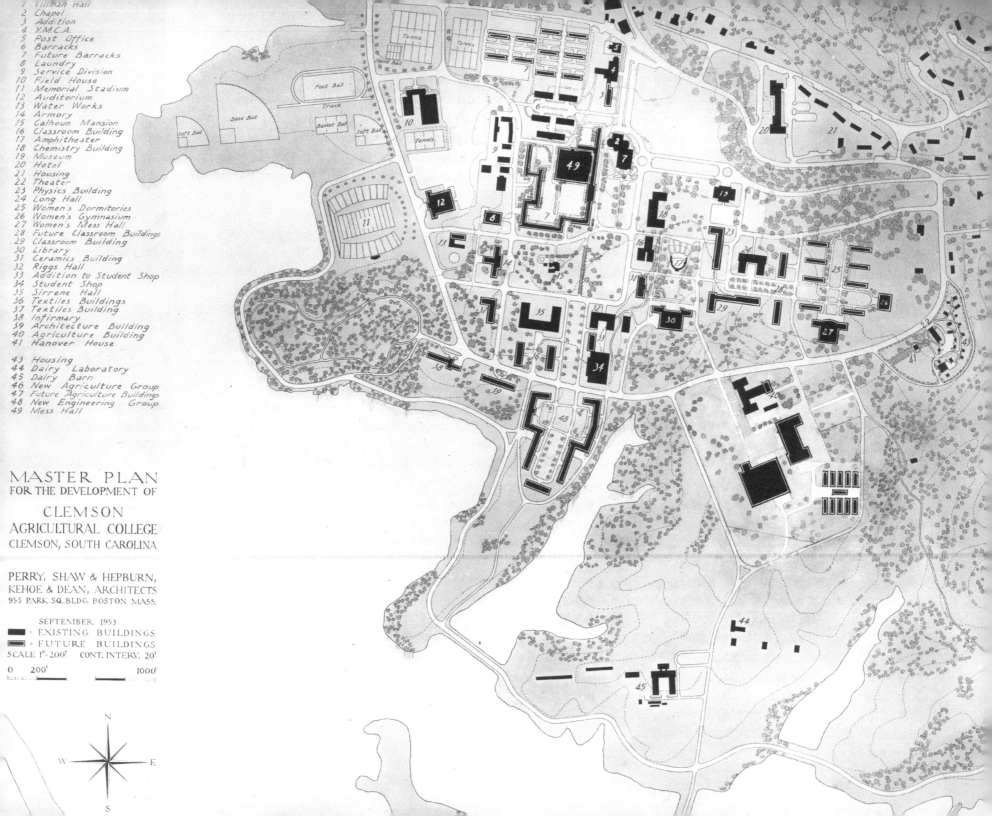

1 Tillman Hall
2 Chapel
3 Addition
4 Y.M.C.A.
5 Post Office
6 Barracks
7 Future Barracks
8 Laundry
9 Service Division
10 Field House
11 Memorial Stadium
12 Auditorium
13 Water Works
14 Armory
15 Calhoun Mansion
16 Classroom Building
17 Amphitheater
18 Chemistry Building
19 Museum
20 Hotel
21 Housing
22 Theater
23 Physics Building
24 Long Hall
25 Women's Dormitories
26 Women's Gymnasium
27 Women's Mess Hall
28 Future Classroom Buildings
29 Classroom Building
30 Library
31 Ceramics Building
32 Riggs Hall
33 Addition to Student Shop
34 Student Shop
35 Sirrene Hall
36 Textiles Buildings
37 Textiles Building
38 Infirmary
39 Architecture Building
40 Agriculture Building
41 Hanover House

43 Housing
44 Dairy Laboratory
45 Dairy Barn
46 New Agriculture Group
47 Future Agriculture Buildings
48 New Engineering Group
49 Mess Hall

MASTER PLAN
FOR THE DEVELOPMENT OF

CLEMSON
AGRICULTURAL COLLEGE
CLEMSON, SOUTH CAROLINA

PERRY, SHAW & HEPBURN,
KEHOE & DEAN, ARCHITECTS
955 PARK SQ. BLDG. BOSTON MASS.

SEPTEMBER 1953
= EXISTING BUILDINGS
= FUTURE BUILDINGS
SCALE 1"-200' CONT. INTERV. 20'

0   200'   1000'

N
W   E
S

CLEMSON UNIVERSITY MASTER PLAN

FIG. 2-3
*Campus Master
Plan, PSHKD*

FIG. 2-4 *Master
Plan 3-D Model*

McClure took the lead in campus planning and proposed to Edwards the creation of new "master planning studies" to supplement the master plan of 1953, which he called a "skeleton" that provided a "logical generalized location pattern for building groups," but used inaccurate and incomplete site data.[24] Edwards agreed and the master plan that resulted in 1960 used a novel approach to campus development by arranging buildings, traffic patterns, and landscape planning in three dimensions;[25] McClure and his staff adroitly moved or added buildings as necessary to the large model located outside McClure's office. That practice continued until Edwards called for a ten-year master plan in 1966, a written document that listed planned buildings, their completion dates, and estimates of cost.[26] It, along with the plans of 1960 and 1953, were followed so assiduously that

eventually almost everything projected was built. Those buildings shown as "future" in 1953 were eventually constructed (although not always on the exact sites indicated), while those that went unbuilt (an addition to the YMCA, a water works plant, an armory, a museum, and an additional textile building) were no longer considered priorities. Buildings projected by the master plan model of 1960, which appeared in photographs and, after construction, on campus maps, depicted buildings that exemplified modern campus planning in style and spirit. However, notably absent were three exponents of the period—THE MULTI-PURPOSE AUDITORIUM, THE CONTINUING EDUCATION CENTER, AND THE STROM THURMOND DEVELOPMENT.

HARLAN EWART MCCLURE

During his illustrious career as an architect, educator, and artist, Harlan McClure produced designs of government and academic buildings, churches, and private residences that earned numerous accolades: the Topaz Medallion, for excellence in architectural education from the American Institute of Architects; the Order of the Palmetto, for service to the state of South Carolina; and the Verner Award, for contributions to the fine arts in South Carolina.

McClure began his teaching career at the University of Minnesota in 1945. After earning his graduate degree in architecture from MIT, he accepted the position of head of the Department of Architecture at Clemson University in 1955 and was appointed as Dean when the College of Architecture was created in 1958. McClure founded the Clemson Architectural Foundation, which is considered by many as one of the most successful support foundations in the country for the building profession. His efforts brought nationally and internationally renowned architects and artists to campus, and his global perspective, and desire to enrich the student educational experience, birthed the Charles E. Daniel Center for Building Research and Urban Studies in Genoa, Italy. Since its establishment in 1973, the Center has provided hundreds of students and alumni the opportunity to study abroad. Although McClure's death in 2001 ended his prodigious accomplishments, his observable campus legacy, Lee and Lowry halls, stand as but one example of his outstanding Modernist designs.

THE DESIGN OF THE PERIOD that perhaps most epitomized modernity, in the end the Multi-purpose Auditorium evolved into a structure that performed the function sought, but bore no resemblance to the original design. It exhibited no hallmarks of the period; rather, the constraints of operating within an unalterable budget produced the result. The project sprung primarily from the need for a venue to host athletic events, as the College increased the variety of sports offered and the numbers who attended grew.[27] There were also other activities to accommodate, such as concerts, dances, intramural contests, and class registration. The "big gym" used at the time lacked sufficient lighting and proper ventilation (made worse by smoking, which was permitted) and could not accommodate large numbers of people.[28]

A new structure to host campus events—a combined auditorium and coliseum—was projected in the master plan of 1953, but disagreements over the architects' plans prompted several alternative options: one combined a coliseum and armory; one paired the auditorium with a student union center; another combined the coliseum with an auditorium and chapel, and still another combined an armory and student union building. Professor Glenn, who had supervised the construction of Memorial Stadium in 1942, evaluated the options and presented his recommendation to President Poole: "Due to structural reasons we believe that a combined armory and student union building would fit more economically than any other combination of purposes. The combined armory and student union building would not require near the extensive parking space required for an auditorium or coliseum." From his investigations of other academic institutions, Glenn learned that retractable seating increased the versatility of the space, making it usable for commencement exercises, dances, and other athletic events. The building committee, which included President Poole, concluded that "a combination auditorium and coliseum and a combined armory and student union building would meet the needs at Clemson for some years to come;" this had the advantage of not requiring extensive parking space, an issue of increasing concern.[29]

In 1963 President Edwards and University of South Carolina President Thomas F. Jones expressed the needs of both institutions for a "multi-purpose building" for their respective campuses, that included "provisions for playing basketball."[30] They drafted reports to the state legislature's Ways and Means Committee to determine how to obtain funds for construction, but the committee did not request an appropriation until 1965 when it considered the matter again. Almost immediately the *Greenville News* voiced its opposition to the legislation with an editorial, "Coliseum Issue Rising Again," which expressed the view that the funds called for by the proposed legislation could be better used for academic purposes; interestingly, the newspaper objected to the proposed facility only at South Carolina, not Clemson.[31] In spite of the newspaper's views, South Carolina H-1613 was passed by both the House and Senate, and was signed into law in May 1965.[32]

The legislation authorized Clemson University to construct "a multi-purpose auditorium and other facilities" estimated at $2 million each, and the University of South Carolina a "large building (now under design)" estimated at $4 million.[33] To finance the projects, the legislation advanced $2 million to each institution (to be repaid by admission charges and student fees). The remainder was to be raised by the institutions themselves, obtained through gift, grant, or issuance of other bonds. As provided for in the legislation, President Edwards recommended charging an admission fee for all performances, contests, and events occurring in the facility, and a fee of $2.50 per student, per semester, to remain in effect for as long as necessary to repay the full amount of the sum paid by the State. He also recommended that the administration be authorized and directed to develop plans, select architects, determine timing, and implement plans for the funding of construction. The Trustees agreed.[34]

Immediately after the legislation passed, Hassie Forrester of the J. E. Sirrine Company, an established architectural and engineering firm founded by Joseph Emory Sirrine in 1921, contacted President Edwards to express interest in the project. The head of Sirrine's design group, Charles Bates, was a Clemson architecture alumnus of 1953. Bates had worked on the design team for the Charlotte Coliseum and Auditorium and headed the design team for the Baltimore Civic Center, and was thus well qualified. In addition to Bates, Forrester further outlined that the Sirrine staff consisted of forty-four architects, engineers, and draftsmen as well as 221 other individuals concerned with "heavy process installations" who could complete the work with "competence and dispatch."[35] The J. E. Sirrine Company had planned and constructed textile mills, primarily in the Carolinas, as well as buildings on the Clemson campus.[36] It was unsurprising that Clemson, a national leader in textile education, chose the company to complete the design.

FIG. 2-5 *Littlejohn Coliseum*

When the news became public, the heads of the departments of animal, dairy, and poultry science contacted President Edwards via Dean J. K. Williams, to express the desire of College of Agricultural and Biological Sciences faculty for a livestock pavilion in the multi-purpose building. The group pointed out that the need for such a pavilion had existed since 1959 for events such as horse shows and 4-H and Future Farmers of America contests; short courses in dehorning and branding and other dairy management practices; sales events; and meetings of veterinary science groups.[37] There is no record that President Edwards responded to the issues raised by the agriculture faculty; in his view the function of the new facility had not been determined. At least in statements to the press, Edwards commented only that he saw "physical training" as "one of most critical needs," and that "recent newspaper accounts describing what is to be built on this campus have been entirely erroneous."[38]

To sort out the issues related to the structure's purpose, construction, and financing, Edwards appointed a "Special Committee on Planning Student Recreation Facilities." Their findings, issued in July 1965, stated that the most urgent need was a physical recreation building and a multi-purpose coliseum (a change in terminology) that would "accommodate large crowds for any number of various activities."[39] The committee recommended the construction of two facilities: one, a physical recreation facility of 80,000 square feet located east of Williamson Road, north of the Physical Plant buildings, and in the general area of the present varsity field; and the other, a multi-purpose coliseum with an arena and seating for 12,500, to be used for convocations, basketball games, concerts, expositions, and other university activities requiring significant space and seating capacity, on a location west of "A" Street and "in the general area of the old National Guard Armory."[40] The committee also recommended that different architects be engaged for these two projects and President Edwards agreed, but called for the elimination of an eight-lane bowling alley from the physical recreation facility because he thought the space could be used for other more practical reasons. Edwards concluded his letter: "I think it is extremely important that we have a clear understanding as to the cost estimates for these projects before plans and specifications progress too far."[41]

CHARLES LYMAN BATES

"I was bombarded with questions about the roof," Charles Bates said when recounting the details of the design of the Multipurpose Auditorium. The tetrahedron roof, also called a "space frame," unlike anything used on a Clemson University building in 1967, generated a variety of reactions. Some, unhappy with the design, thought it "too radical" for Clemson and questioned its use of Cor-Ten steel, an alloy which oxidized into a stable rusted brown finish that eliminated the need for painting. So, to settle doubts about using the steel, Bates and Ralph Collins, chair of the building committee, traveled to Chicago to meet with executives of US Steel. At that meeting, the two men were pointed to a nearby table that held, as Bates recalled, a "chunk of metal" that was Cor-Ten steel and had been used by the artist Pablo Picasso for his famous monumental sculpture "Chicago Picasso," which stands today in Daley Plaza. Upon their return to Clemson Bates and Collins reported their findings, Collins still opposed to using the steel, but Bates strongly in favor of its appropriateness for his design. Bates prevailed.

A native of Elkin, North Carolina, Bates received his degree in architecture from Clemson in 1953. An eight year stint with A. G. Odell, Jr. Associates In Charlotte, NC, followed by two years with J. E. Sirrene Company in Greenville, South Carolina, produced many memorable buildings: the Charlotte Coliseum, Wachovia Bank high-rise headquarters, Church of the Holy Comforter (Belmont, North Carolina), Baltimore Civic Center, St. Francis Hospital, and the Greenville News-Piedmont building. In 1966 Bates set up practice in Hilton Head and for the next sixteen

SB 2-3 *Bates*

years produced over 300 designs for projects that included the Hyatt Hotel in Palmetto Dunes, a fire station, Tom Fazio Golf Villas, the Hilton Head airport, and numerous private homes.

Bates died June 3, 2020, leaving a rich architectural heritage. His lasting contributions to modernist architecture continue to inspire.

FIG. 2-6 *Multipurpose Auditorium Color Rendering*

After Edwards appointed the building committee for the Physical Recreation Building, chaired by Ralph Collins, head of the Physical Plant division,[42] there exists little evidence that the group met or that architects were commissioned for the project. We know only that Sirrine engineers called for the development of site plans for the two projects specified by the legislative act, as well as buildings proposed for varsity athletics and fine arts.[43] Sirrine's Forrester wrote Collins that the company wanted both facilities designed through the schematic stage so that proper site planning of both buildings could be accomplished simultaneously.[44] But Collins, in what was a test of the integrity of master planning, replied that these structures "should be made in accordance with the University's Master Plan for the Campus" (Clemson earned university status in 1964) and that McClure and his staff were studying sites for these facilities; he also notified others, perhaps as advance warning, that any plans would be "determined in conjunction with overall planning."[45] Aside from the issue of site plans, Forrester's letter to Collins also raised a red flag concerning cost; he expressed concern about restrictions imposed by the fixed amount of $2 million to carry out Bates's design.

The design produced by Bates incorporated, in the words of President Edwards, "the best features which could be combined in our building" gathered from committee visits to major auditoriums and coliseums.[46] Bates, a student of the modern idiom from his work at Odell Associates in Charlotte, North Carolina, produced a tour de force design in glass and steel for a structure that contained over 88,000 square feet, with 10,228 permanent seats and over 600 bleacher seats ringing the basketball floor. Half of the seating, constructed of hardwood and wrought iron, was below ground. The crowning feature of the design—the roof, supported underneath a geometric tetrahedron truss system, commonly called a space frame, 351 feet square—was supported by eight columns located at the perimeter of the structural system, all with the goal of eliminating structural steelwork and exposed steel framing. The roof itself, made of exposed Cor-ten steel, was cantilevered twenty-seven feet around the entire building and created an immense space free from interior supports.[47] Its innovative design required additional engineering expertise from Engineers Collaborative of Chicago, which came at an additional cost.[48]

*Edwards showing
Multipurpose Auditorium*

Members of the building committee immediately expressed their concern over the Cor-ten steel, which was a "new steel" developed to be used without painting, that oxidized to a reddish-brown finish. Collins, as chair, echoed the sentiments of committee members:

> Mr. Young's [Joe Young, one of the committee members] expression of concern was not of engineering and structural problems but the possible acceptance of this radically new idea being used on our Campus. However, it was pointed out by our architects that such a structure as large as this one would, by necessity, have different architectural features from anything on the Campus now.[49]

Bates attempted to educate the building committee on the advantages of the tetrahedron roof and Cor-ten steel, and was "bombarded" with questions about his design,[50] which was released to the press and publicly displayed by President Edwards during halftime at a basketball game in January 1966. At that time, the announcement stated that bids for the $2 million project would begin in May, with the awarding of the contract in July. Newspapers carried the story along with Bates's color rendering showing the sleek glass façade. But a month later, after receiving questions from the building committee about the amount of glass used, Bates recommended substituting marble in lieu of glass on the upper portion of the exterior façade:

> Please note the band of glass at podium level which is a combination of exit doors and fixed glass panels. . . . The low glass, with lighting at night, will permit the visual motion of people on the interior concourse and enhance the appearance . . . I will present to you a typical sample of the Georgia White Cherokee Marble [sic] on my next trip to Clemson.[51]

The marble alternative, however, proved too costly and was rejected.

By May, Bates had contacted Engineers Collaborative about "exceeded budget design" concerning the joint details and erection methods of the tetrahedron frame.[52] The engineers had already begun to study the possibility of a new vertical truss design, column details, caisson foundations, and spread footings to cut costs, but Bates nevertheless projected that all bid documents would be completed by mid-June and that bids could be taken in July 1966:

> Please be assured of my continued interest in detail refinements, however, it is my firm conviction that your and my obligation is to the Clemson University officials who established a budget which we verified to be sufficient. As a matter of fact, this challenge will ultimately determine if we're the engineer and architect <u>we</u> <u>think</u> we are.[53] (original emphasis)

Collins, who was not a fan of the roof and sought any measures to cut costs, wrote the building committee with foreboding news:

> Our commissioned architects-engineers continue to wrestle with the problems of design and cost of the steel frame. . . . As of May 24th, and after some discussions with Mr. [Mel] Wilson and Dean McClure, I asked the commissioned architects to consider, by developing some elevation sketches, etc., the removal of the overhang from around the periphery of the building. The estimators indicated that this overhang is worth approximately $200,000 and that its deletion may accrue a net savings of $175,000. With so much money involved, it seems wise to investigate all other possibilities. . . . We will expect a full committee meeting to consider the above questions of possible deletion of the overhang as soon as we have sufficient information.[54]

FIG. 2-8 *Littlejohn Coliseum, 1969*

Two days later, Collins wrote that Bates presented cost estimates of various architectural and structural schemes, including the tetrahedron space frame with overhang. The death knell had sounded for Bates's design:

> The Building Committee was unanimous in its conclusion that the scheme of using a Vertical Truss Frame [sic] enclosed on all sides, with the roof deck on top, was the most acceptable based on estimated cost. This scheme of engineering and architecture would delete the overhanging portion of the space frame. The estimated cost differential between this scheme and the original was estimated between $300,000 and $337,000. It was also the unanimous opinion . . . that the architects should pursue this method with diligence.[55]

Collins concluded by commending the Sirrine Company for presenting complete and thorough information which permitted the Building Committee "to make a responsible decision for the University."[56] The resulting structure, Littlejohn Coliseum, bore no resemblance to Bates's design and was DEDICATED ON FEBRUARY 22, 1969.[57]

THE CONTINUING EDUCATION Center (CEC) project, which followed a few years after the Multi-purpose Auditorium, was also tethered to state appropriations—but when the State Budget and Control Board entirely eliminated those funds, the CEC succumbed. Though abolishing the budget was ostensibly the chief cause of death, other factors related to campus development contributed to the project's demise.

CONTINUING EDUCATION CENTER

1972

Campus enrollment, the catalyst for campus planning, in large part also dictated the construction agenda. Thus the decision of the Trustees, using guidance provided by CMP consultants, to maintain enrollment at 10,000 students meant that housing and other variables such as dining and parking could be predicted and controlled, which, in turn, allowed implementation of the construction agenda prescribed by the campus master plans of 1953, 1960, and 1966. Those plans, however, did not address the "critical parking situation" that both Presidents Poole and Edwards had identified and sought to resolve. At last, in 1969 Edwards instructed Wright Bryan, the soon-to-retire Vice-president for Development, and Dean McClure to develop a master plan for parking.[58] Instead, what resulted was a proposal to create an official position of Campus Master Planner that vested the Vice-president for Development with authority to approve expenditures, and the Dean of the School of Architecture with "professional direction" of the Master Planning Office.[59] Locating future buildings became the responsibility of the new master planner, while implementing the plans became the job of the Vice-president for Business and Finance; creation of working drawings was assigned to the Physical Plant. The proposal further directed the Master Planning Office to continue developing and updating the campus plan model and the display of photos and drawings of campus development, located in Lee Hall.[60] But after Bryan retired in 1970 the new Vice-president of Development, Stan Nicholas, opposed the Bryan-McClure plan. With the backing of President Edwards, Nicholas restructured the reporting lines of the master planning staff, architects, and physical plant staff, terminated existing appointments to all planning and building committees, and "reconstituted" all other committees deemed "necessary."[61]

As the changes were made and implemented in 1972, Clemson requested permanent improvements for fiscal year 1973–74 to convert Clemson House into a continuing education center, which Edwards called "a necessity if South Carolina hoped to attract high-intensity industries,"[62] because it afforded leaders in business and industry opportunities to stay abreast of developments through short courses and seminars. Edwards had analyzed the projected increases in the number of continuing education programs offered by each of the nine colleges in specialized laboratories already on campus and informed the Trustees: "There is absolutely no doubt in my mind that this university will have more activity in this area [continuing education] than is represented by the entire student body."[63] Support for the CEC also came from Governor John C. West, who proposed to use $6 million of the state surplus for capital improvements, and other funds from the general appropriations bill of 1973–74 authorized the construction of meeting rooms, a registration lobby, and ancillary functions.[64] When news of the proposed CEC became public, several architects contacted President Edwards seeking consideration for the project. Since no established procedures for selecting architectural and engineering firms for state projects existed, the State Budget and Control Board directed the creation of formal procedures to ensure competition. These new procedures directed state agencies to hold conferences with at least three firms submitting resumes, select the three which were the most qualified, and submit the names to the Board with supporting documentation.[65] The new process granted the Board authority to designate which firm would be used, and gave it the right to reject the entire list submitted.[66]

ROBERT C. EDWARDS

Edwards's vision of a modern university manifested itself in fifty-eight new buildings and additions which all reflected a contemporary style; these included a library, classroom buildings, twelve dormitories, a health center, and an arena for athletic events. Although he frequently spoke about the campus "building program," Edwards did not dwell on the subject of campus planning; nevertheless, when he established the office of campus master planner and named Robert Eflin to the post in 1973, Edwards secured the place of modern campus planning at Clemson University.

The eighth president of Clemson University, Edwards entered Clemson College at the age of fifteen and received his degree in textile engineering in 1933. He continued his career in textiles at plants in the Carolinas and Virginia where he worked in quality control and management positions.

In 1956 Edwards was named Vice-President for Development at Clemson College and took charge of campus planning and development activities. Upon the sudden death of President Robert F. Poole in 1958, Edwards began his twenty-year presidential tenure which was characterized by vigor and imagination. The Edwards years ushered in a modern university having an expanded physical plant, a growing curriculum, a diverse student body, and a change in name from "college" to "university" that more accurately described the modern institution.

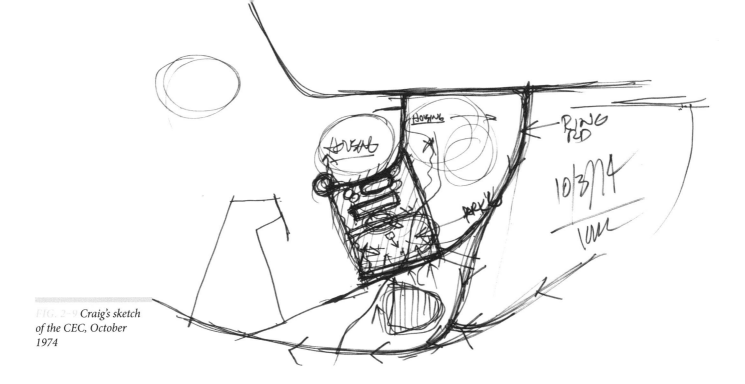

FIG. 2-9 *Craig's sketch of the CEC, October 1974*

With the funding appropriation on track for approval, President Edwards in March 1974 appointed the building committee. It consisted of twenty-one members, two being students, and another being Campus Master Planner Robert Eflin, hired in 1973 and the first to hold that title.[67] In June Kirk Craig, the architect selected for the project, gave a broad brush presentation of the requirements and basic area allocations for the center, the cost of which he estimated initially at $10 million. Craig presented a tentative outline for the development of the contract documents, schematics, and working drawings (but no formal renderings), with reviews, bidding, and acceptance of contract to be completed by the end of June 1975. The minutes of the meeting recorded the ambitious timetable:

This highly optimistic schedule was discussed in detail and every effort will be made by the committee to comply with the architect's request for information and to render decisions at appropriate times. It was the concern of the architect and the chairman that some slippage should be built into the schedule and that this target date would be difficult to achieve if the review, bidding, and contract acceptance phase of the project takes a full 90 days.[68]

Seven sites were considered for the Center, but the site favored by architects Craig and Gaulden, located just south of the R. M. Cooper Library,[69] raised concerns and elicited discussion because it could not provide necessary parking. Craig recommended peripheral parking for the large number of people that would attend events, and the committee referred the matter to Eflin for further study and resolution.[70]

KIRK CRAIG AND
EARLE GAULDEN

Kirk Craig and Earle Gaulden first met when they were students at Clemson in the late 1950s studying architecture. Both men left South Carolina to pursue graduate degrees in architecture, Craig to Harvard and Gaulden to Georgia Tech. They returned to Greenville in 1957 and launched their trail-blazing partnership. Most people in Upstate South Carolina were familiar with Georgian architecture, but, as Gaulden recounted, "We set out to conquer those prejudices." While Gaulden spent hours at the drafting board, Craig recruited clients. The harmonious relationship lasted more than fifty years, ended only by Craig's passing in 2007.

Craig, the principal architect for the Continuing Education Center at Clemson University in 1974, is often cited for "Kirk's Paradigm," which is a succinct statement of factors necessary for a successful project: "the right owner, the right program, the right site, the right budget, the right contractor, and the right architect." When applying this paradigm to the Continuing Education Center project, two factors went unmet: the right site and the right budget. Not obtaining the commission for the CEC did not impede the work of the two men, however.

Joined by another Clemson graduate, Bill Davis, the three formed Craig Gaulden Davis in January 1978. Their record of accomplishments includes the Greenville County Museum of Art, the Little Theater, and the Peace Center for the Performing Arts. In 2010 partners of the firm honored the founders with pledges of generous financial support for the expansion, renovation, and restoration of Lee Hall on the Clemson campus.

60

Craig's suggestion to create offsite parking meshed perfectly with Eflin's thinking, which advocated the supremacy of pedestrians, and his stated goal, to make decisions that contributed to the "overall, cohesive continuing development of the University."[71] Those views translated into plans that put the circulation of people, cars, and bicycles in first place. "Traffic and parking" he said, "were confusing and simply a big problem to work with."[72] Eflin's master plan for parking, which Edwards had ordered years earlier, at last addressed the subject comprehensively: it designated planned zones for permanent parking, located lots in areas consistent with expansion plans, eliminated thru traffic from academic areas during the day, and created parking lots with hard surfaces, lighting, and landscaping. The plan ensured that university employees would walk no farther than five minutes to and from their work stations, and that students would walk no more than ten minutes to their classes.[73] Eflin's pedestrian-friendly plan, therefore, did not accommodate the large on-campus parking space needed by the CEC; event attendees would have to park off-campus.

But the State Budget and Control Board had the final say in October 1975 when it recalled the $6 million appropriated to fund the CEC and put plans "on hold;" the surplus which made the funds available had been drained by deficit spending.[74] The possibility of using other funds also came to naught when the Board cut appropriations for general operations by $3 million more,[75] sealing the project's fate. Edwards told the Trustees that the CEC "should be put on the back burner," and discussions about possible sites continued until the end of his presidency in 1979. The two main sites under scrutiny— south of the library and Clemson House (which would have required extensive renovation)—each had support among the Trustees, but the heavily wooded site south of the library remained the favorite in spite of parking difficulties.[76]

President Edwards's successor, Bill Atchley, attempted to breathe new life into the project after he took office in 1979 by speaking of its value to various groups around the state during his "Meet Bill Atchley" junket. The "dueling sites" on which to build the center had divided support among the Trustees, but Vice-president Nicholas recommended hiring "an off-campus third party" to "help finalize the most optimum location."[77] Two site analyses followed, each with different conclusions. The first, in November 1979, used Atchley's own evaluation as a professional engineer and found that the Clemson House site was unacceptable. The other, a marketability study by accountants Laventhol and Horwath, in October 1981, recommended neither site; it identified a location slightly further south, "contiguous to Perimeter Road and proximate to the former University dairy barns . . . and to the area designated as the future development location for the proposed golf course."[78] The General Assembly approved funding to proceed with plans, but was stopped by a gubernatorial veto. President Atchley, "appalled" at the veto, addressed the General Assembly: "it is inconceivable to me that a state, which is as dependent on industry and agriculture as an economic base, can ignore the valuable role of continuing education."[79] Atchley, however, had NO INTENTION OF ABANDONING PLANS FOR THE PROJECT.

FIG. 2-10 *Eflin*

61

THE START OF THE ATCHLEY presidency in 1979 also marked the beginning of the work to create a new campus master plan. The 1960 plan had worked well, until the volume of campus development and renovations accelerated to the point that the Board of Visitors questioned whether McClure and his limited staff could keep pace with making the changes to the model.[80] Unveiled in 1982, the new campus master plan—for the first time published in narrative format—focused on growth and the problems of the modern campus, which campus planners referred to as "cities of learning" because of their similarities to urban living.[81] The plan reflected the hand of Campus Master Planner Eflin in that it asserted the rights of the pedestrian, but also presented ways to develop the shores of Lake Hartwell advantageously. The plan depicted dramatic campus growth in the number of new buildings to be constructed—thirty-six new buildings for academics, housing, and student activities. Other projects slated for construction included an athletic field, golf course, natatorium, chemistry building, policy institute, theater, and continuing education center.

STROM THURMOND DEVELOPMENT
1982

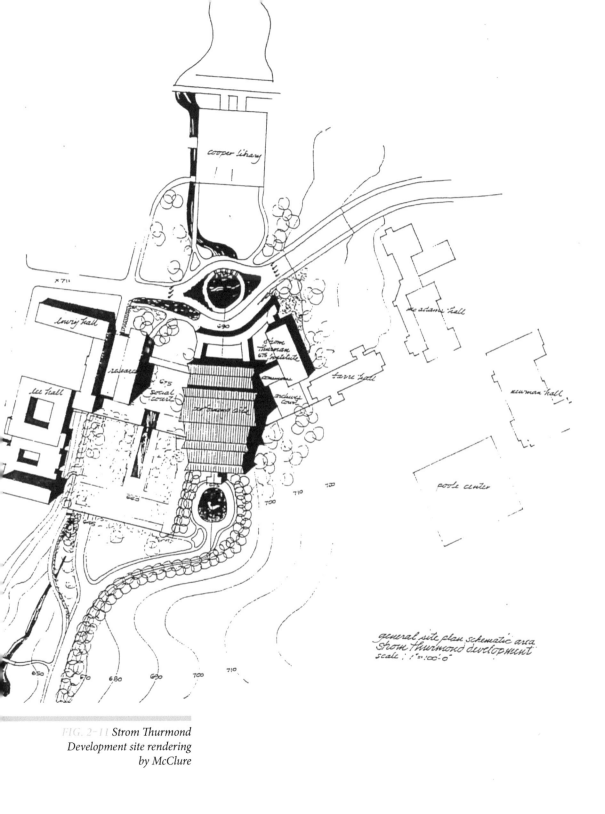

cooper library

x 711

lowry hall

research

lee hall

675
social
court

strom
thurmond
678 institute

continuing
orchard
court

mc adams hall

farre hall

newman hall

poole center

690

700

700

710

700

650   670   680   690   700   710

general site plan schematic area
strom thurmond development
scale : 1"=100'-0"

FIG. 2-11 *Strom Thurmond
Development site rendering
by McClure*

Undeterred by the poor reception accorded the CEC project, President Atchley continued speaking to audiences around the state about Clemson's mission and his plans to create new academic and public service programs that brought nationally-known figures to campus[82]—namely, alumnus Strom Thurmond, who fulfilled Atchley's public service criteria through his lifetime of work as a teacher, public school superintendent, judge, governor, and US senator. Upon passage of a President's Council resolution urging Thurmond to donate his papers, Atchley proposed the creation of a center—a public policy "think tank"—for political research, that he and Political Science Professor Horace Fleming conceptualized in three component parts: the Strom Thurmond Institute, a performing arts center, and a continuing education center. The "Strom Thurmond Development," as rendered by Dean McClure, placed the project within the context of the campus master plan and clearly depicted the Institute, performing arts center, and continuing education center clustered on the site once proposed for the CEC—just south of the R. M. Cooper Library, a site described by Atchley as "a park-like area" that "tied together the backwaters of Lake Hartwell and the very center of the campus."[83]

63

FIG. 2-12 *Site for Strom Thurmond Development (pre-construction)*

FIG. 2-13 *Strom Thurmond Development Buildings, McClure*

Atchley's motivation to honor Thurmond was mixed with his desire to see new campus buildings come to fruition. The Thurmond Center (a term he used for the three new buildings) served, as he expressed bluntly, "as a way to get some things needed on this campus like a performing arts building and a continuing education building. With the economic climate today, I'm not at all sure we could build a performing arts building or a continuing education building without the Thurmond Center approach." That approach involved obtaining funds from the private sector, described by Atchley as "new and exciting ways" to increase the assets of the Clemson University Foundation.[84] But Paul McAlister, speaking for the planning committee of the Trustees, expressed his doubts about

Atchley's use of "innovative means" for obtaining the continuing education center component, which in his view had "priority over all other functions;" he directed Atchley to explore the possibility of constructing the CEC on leased land, without a proposed golf course and residential development.[85] Atchley countered that developers would be sought for the center and the golf course, if it was feasible.[86] But when Campus Planner Mark Wright submitted the cost estimates for "Phase I" of the project a year later, he omitted the CEC and included estimates for the Institute building, performing arts center (at a cost of $2 million more than the Institute), and an underground parking structure estimated at $5 million.[87]

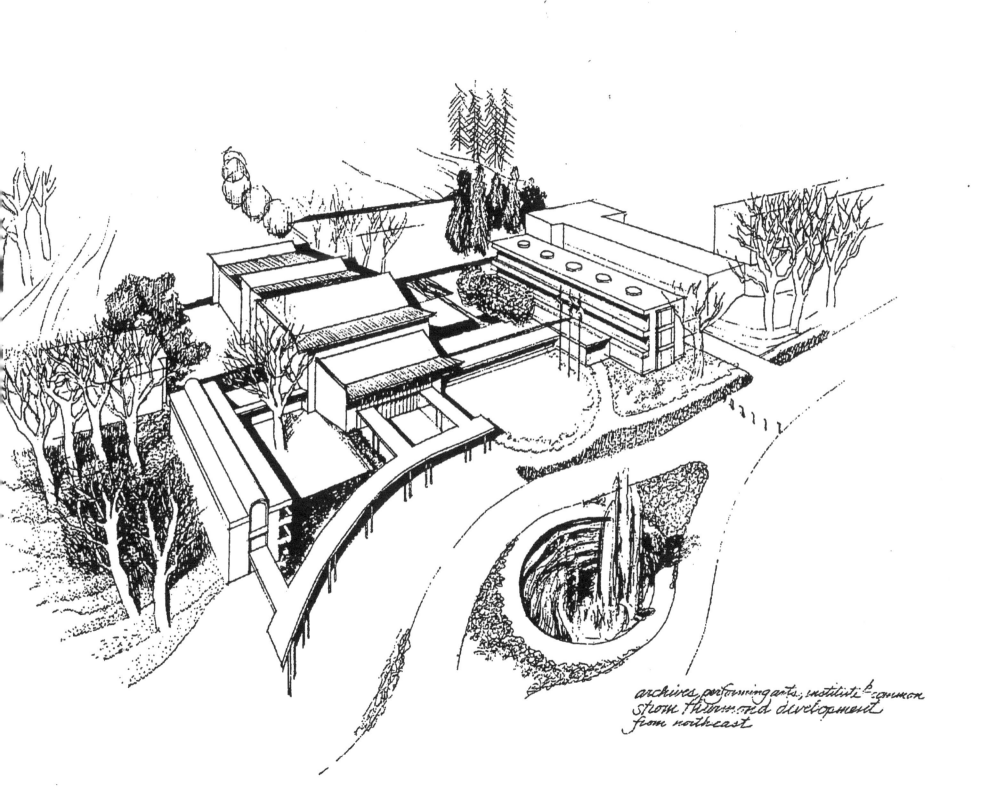

archives, performing arts, institute & common room through development from northeast

FIG. 2–14 Strom Thurmond Development 3-D Model

Fundraising commenced, led by former Texas Governor John Connally and Daniel International Chairman Buck Mickel, but quickly plateaued, failing to achieve the expected results.[88] Because projections for the first phase of fundraising called for $3 million for the Institute and $7 million for the performing arts facility, the building committee, in an effort to boost fundraising, issued "Guidelines for Potential Developers" which invited developers, architects, engineers, investment firms, and real estate firms to submit proposals. In what proved the first of many changes that followed, those guidelines altered the original plan, which placed the CEC in the location indicated by McClure's original schematic, and linked it to the proposed golf course, which was projected in the new campus master plan, near Lake Hartwell.[89] The guidelines stated that the only Clemson resources utilized in the project would be the prime land adjoining the campus specified in "exact arrangements" determined by the South Carolina Attorney General, and that proceeds from townhouses presold to aid in the financing of the project would be incorporated into the golf course, with profits obtained used to help finance the "overall Center."[90]

The Cushman Corporation, a real estate development company based in Atlanta, submitted a proposal using these guidelines in July 1983. The Cushman proposal placed the continuing education center complex farther south near the shores of Lake Hartwell, and broached the prospect of raising funds by selling campus condominiums near the planned golf course. Under this scheme money for construction would have been borrowed from the Founders of the Strom Thurmond Center, then repaid after the sale of the condominiums.[91] Senator Thurmond, Trustee James Waddell, and President Atchley all favored the lake site,[92] but the University Planning Board nixed the plan and recommended that Lockwood Greene Engineers reanalyze the site selection, since such a move would deviate from the campus master plan which the Trustees had approved just months earlier.[93]

In March 1983, the Trustees commissioned Jim Boniface, a consultant and architect who directed master planning efforts, to analyze the various options and recommend the most desirable site for the Thurman development. Boniface, who essentially agreed with Atchley, stated at the outset his intent to use the campus master plan to evaluate each option, a practice that universities nationwide were exploring as they worked with the private sector to fund academic needs. Said Boniface: "With the financial pressures of today, the idea is to find a way the university can use available resources—land, in Clemson's case—to produce funds for new programs."[94] Boniface's analysis of three sites recommended "Plan B," which separated the components by placing the Institute building near campus (the original site south of Cooper Library), the performing arts center farther to the south, and the continuing education center and golf course on the shores of Lake Hartwell.[95]

With the site finalized and fundraising underway but still well below the target amount, in January 1985 Enwright Associates released a new design that depicted an Institute building and a continuing education building, but not a performing arts center.[96] The design featured amphitheater-like colonnades, a plaza roof, and a three-story tower (the focal point) which rested on the plaza roof; the design did not "respect existing campus axes," commented the campus master planner, but it "stood in refreshing contrast to them."[97] The Trustees, hoping to construct the continuing education building as part of the group, voted in July to request the General Assembly to include $5 million in the bond bill for that purpose,[98] and although a Senate panel approved the legislation, Governor Riley vetoed the project along with four other similar state projects. Ultimately the General Assembly overrode the veto and approved the funding for the continuing education building, but two years passed before it became available.[99] Because of the delay, and in need of funds so that groundbreaking could begin on schedule, the architects again revised the design. The pared down result, which changed the grounds around the building and removed the central rotunda and tower that would have housed Thurmond's office, successfully cut expenses by $1 million.[100] Construction began in January 1988 and the building was dedicated the following year. The other components of the original Strom Thurmond Development design followed in the locations that Boniface had recommended in 1984: the Brooks Center for the Performing Arts, south of the Institute, was completed in 1994, and the Madren Conference Center on Lake Hartwell in 1995.

In retrospect the Strom Thurmond Development, as originally conceived with its three components, proved too ambitious an undertaking given the site and the available funding. Yet the project helped to distinguish Clemson's modernization period from other eras of campus development in several ways. First, the project accommodated itself to the campus master plan, not conversely, thus respecting its integrity in providing for campus expansion in all directions to accommodate historic growth. Also, the unique architectural style of the project, which abandoned the Collegiate Gothic style used by Bruce and Morgan and the Italianate reinterpretation used by Lee, marked the culmination of the phase of development termed "mosaic."[101] That phase attempted to tie the old to the new, rather than follow a trend that made buildings "stand free from their neighbors."[102] This eclectic approach, which embraced changes happening in education brought about by science, technology, and an evolving campus population, also confronted other troublesome issues such as parking, which had become the controlling design element.[103] Moreover, faced with the realities of financing campus projects, planners and administrators were forced to radically alter or reject designs on the basis of cost. In the end the Strom Thurmond Development, although not constructed as conceived, employed a method of financing that leveraged valuable resources and assets, THEREBY SETTING A NEW PRECEDENT FOR FUNDING CONSTRUCTION.

CHAPTER THREE

VISIONARY PARTNERSHIPS

1990–2014

THE UNBUILT PROJECTS OF THE last decade of the twentieth century and the first decade of the twenty-first may be described as "visionary partnerships," because the projects reflected wisdom and imaginative thinking in partnering with others to ensure Clemson's institutional viability and economic competitiveness. Economic trends that began the 1980s continued into the new century, all of which impacted institutions of higher learning: global competition in manufacturing and trade; a shift of formerly American industry to the developing world; new regional "pockets of progress" within US industry; declining profitability for small farms; and the growth of entrepreneurship and small businesses. In 1986 the Southern Growth Policies Board, a public research agency governed and supported by southern states to promote economic development of the region, called upon higher education institutions to strengthen their economic development role and increase the South's capacity to generate and use technology.[1] The South Carolina Commission on Higher Education, acting on that call, instituted a program for excellence called "the Cutting Edge," which served as the mandate for President Max Lennon to articulate his vision for the University. Called the Second Century, Lennon's initiative was a plan to achieve academic excellence and institutional growth.

Second Century covered five major areas: agriculture and food, engineering and basic science, marketing and management, textiles, and quality of life;[2] within each area specific programs were targeted for growth. While Second Century also advocated recruiting newly emerging industries as university partners and identified internal and external factors that might present opportunities for fledgling partnerships, the basic priorities remained undergraduate and graduate education, research, and service. These ideas became the nucleus of a new campus master plan, commissioned by the Trustees in 1992.[3] Produced by Wallace Roberts and Todd and Frederic Harris Associates, the plan addressed Lennon's goal of increased enrollment by expanding the concepts of land use, facilities, landscape development, and traffic circulation, which had been expressed in the master plan of 1981. The 1992 plan also tackled increasingly complex issues of campus growth that were expected in coming decades, including demolitions, add-ons, renovations, restorations, and space reassignments.[4] Once again the plan addressed the troublesome issue of parking, BUT IN A NEW WAY.

PARKING DECKS

1992, 2002

The advent of the automobile on college and university campuses after World War II and the increased mobility of college populations marked the beginning of a host of problems. Students, employees, and visitors drove cars. Photographs of the Clemson campus during the late 1940s and 1950s show cars parked alongside roads and in virtually any spot they could fit, whether at athletic events or during class periods. When President Robert C. Edwards called for the parking problem to be addressed in 1966, parking lots became the solution, as land was plentiful.[5] As enrollment increased (bringing with it more student drivers) and new buildings required more acreage, planners revisited the problem time and again. Nationally, college planners treated parking in various ways: camouflaging parking lots with trees and shrubs, fitting parking into the "local ambience" by using architectural screens or design elements, or switching from parallel to angled parking.[6] In urban settings planners confined parking to an area with a small footprint and built upward, creating parking garages or parking decks.[7] This option was the subject of ongoing study by Clemson planners.

FIG. 3-1
Parking Decks Map

The campus master plan of 1992 addressed parking comprehensively. Using the "Ten Principals of Parking" issued by the Clemson University Parking Task Force, the master plan espoused "a neighborhood philosophy," rather than a "perimeter philosophy" in determining parking locations. The plan defined a parking garage as a "parking facility" or an "interim destination, serving only as a place for the motorist to leave his or her car before continuing to a final destination usually within a ten minute walk." The plan specified the criteria for selecting sites for parking garages: pedestrian access, vehicular ingress, land use compatibility, topography, and potential for expansion. It also acknowledged that other factors, such as grade differentials or sloping topography, afforded opportunities for efficient use of parking structure sites, noting that erecting structures on sloping terrain would allow construction "without the attendant requirements of lighting and ventilation." The 1992 plan identified three campus sites meeting the criteria for a parking structure—a surface lot west of Memorial Stadium, a site north of the motor pool, and a surface lot adjacent to Sirrine Hall. It outlined construction strategies for the structures, chiefly, that they should be able to accommodate adding more levels as needed, or be located off-site.[8]

Ten years later the campus master plan of 2002, completed by the firm Dober Lidsky and Craig, expanded the 1992 plan by identifying five sites for parking decks.[9] The proposed locations, adjacent to Sirrine Hall, the Brooks Center, east of the Clemson House, east of the Hendrix Center, and off Perimeter Road south of Woodland Cemetery, each allowed a five-minute walk to one's destination. The plan mentioned, but did not indicate on the map, the site next to Memorial Stadium, which was recommended in the 1992 plan. Both the master plan of 1992 and 2002 planned decks for appropriate locations and avoided what campus planning pioneer Richard Dober called the "one deadly sin" in campus design: "the presence of parking in the wrong location."[10] So why weren't the decks built? The short answer: cost. The gain of parking spaces, when weighed against construction costs, could not significantly justify the expenditure, EVEN WITH GRANTS OF FINANCIAL ASSISTANCE.[11]

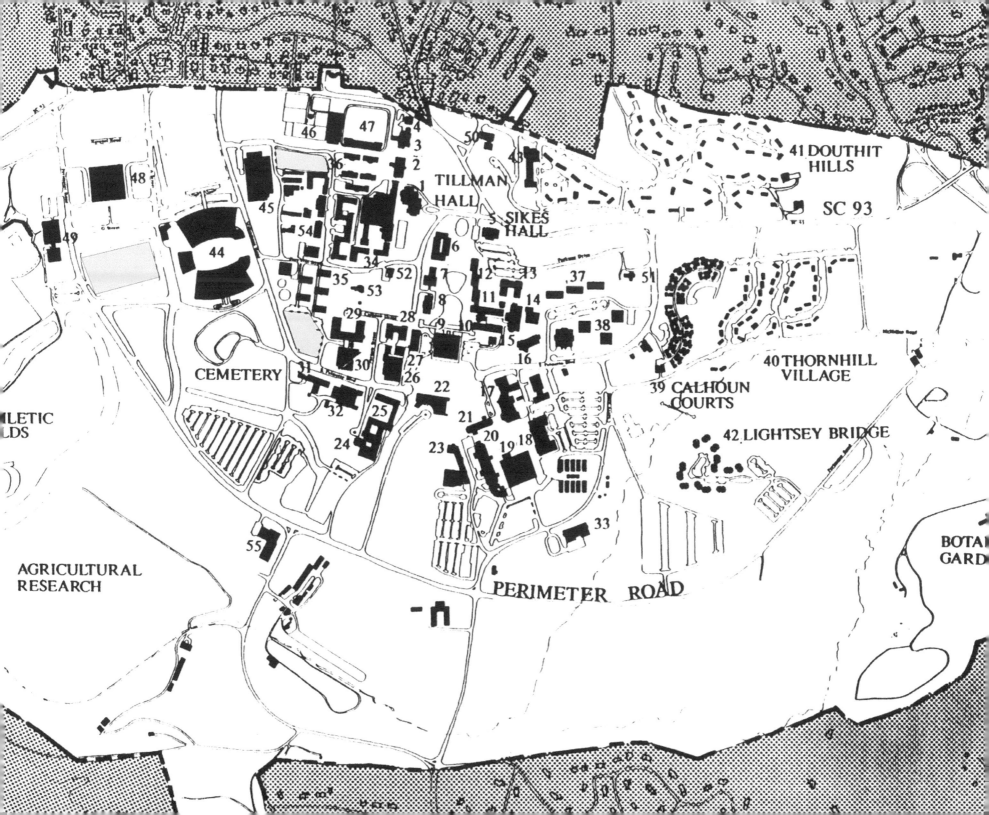

46
47
4
3
2
36
48
45
54
44
49
34
52
35
53
29
28
30
27
26
32
25
24
31
22
21
23
20
19 18
33

TILLMAN HALL
50
48
5 SIKES HALL
6
7
12
13
37
11
14
51
8
9 10
5
38
16
17

55

CEMETERY

ATHLETIC FIELDS

AGRICULTURAL RESEARCH

PERIMETER ROAD

41 DOUTHIT HILLS

SC 93

40 THORNHILL VILLAGE

39 CALHOUN COURTS

42 LIGHTSEY BRIDGE

BOTANICAL GARDEN

WHILE CONTINUING THE construction of parking decks would have changed the rural character and feel of the campus, the creation of parking areas changed the campus even more. There were numerous ripple effects impacting the layout of buildings and precincts, the circulation of pedestrians and cars, and the need to address contaminated runoff from large expanses of asphalt. But not all of the effects created by parking lots were negative.

BOTANICAL GARDEN CONSERVATORY
1994

When Memorial Stadium was expanded in 1959 to create additional parking for fans, a collection of camellias on the site that President Robert Franklin Poole had once proposed as a naturalist park was relocated to an area off Highway 76 on the fringe of campus. That move marked the beginning of what would become the South Carolina Botanical Garden. Originally called the "Ornamental Grounds" and later the "Horticultural Gardens" by the Department of Horticulture, the area served as an outdoor laboratory for teaching and research programs of the department.[12] A 1984 assessment of the gardens recommended the creation of a mission statement to develop the garden, forestry arboretum, and greenspan property (about thirty acres of undeveloped property set aside for recreation).[13] Two years later, faculty in the Department of Biological Sciences, Horticulture and Forestry proposed to President Lennon the creation of a botanical garden and a museum located contiguous to the gardens that would "transcend departmental lines." Their proposal included a planetarium, museum, library, continuing education center, greenhouse, and laboratories;[14] although not built, the project served to stimulate interest in the gardens.

With the kickoff of the "Campaign for Clemson" in 1987 to raise $62 million for new facilities and equipment, President Lennon (with encouragement from his wife, Ruth, a garden enthusiast) appointed a master plan steering committee to develop what was now 208 acres to its maximum potential.[15] The master plan, rendered by Gerald Vander Mey and the steering committee in 1989, included several notable elements, among them an education center which would serve as the nucleus of the garden, an adjacent conservatory to house special collections of rare and exotic species, an ornamental field research area, and a new location for Hanover House. In concept, the conservatory was planned as a "retreat for people to observe the botanical universe"[16] in a lush, exotic environment as a cohesive series of outdoor rooms, or zones: aquatic, floral, tropical, and native.[17] Its 40,000 square feet provided space for garden administrative offices, a permanent plant collection, and education facilities.[18] The conservatory would have comprised half of the facility's total square footage, all contained within a "highly visible and memorable" exterior, at least three-quarters glass or other translucent material.[19] As pictured in the campus master plan, the conservatory occupied the place of preeminence at the breakpoint of the long ridge in the central part of the garden, overlooking a creek running through the Schoenike Arboretum,[20] taking up sixty-five acres in a visually dominant site within the garden. As stated at the time, the presence of a conservatory in this location proclaimed "Clemson's commitment to scientific and aesthetic arts."[21]

Fundraising for the conservatory commenced soon after the garden master plan was published. Led by Tee Senn, former head of the Department of Horticulture, and assisted by David Bradshaw, the garden's first director, and John Kelly, professor and second director of the garden, the campaign raised almost $50,000 by 1991. That amount, supplemented by limited state funds, proved sufficient to hire an architect to design the conservatory and visitor's center.[22] A promising partnership with McDonald's Corporation called for developing a simulated rainforest as part of the conservatory and cultivating vegetables for use in menu offerings, a result that would have given Clemson "one of the most unique teaching and research facilities in the world."[23] But when that partnership failed to coalesce, attention turned toward other ways to raise funds. A boost came when the garden acquired the title and distinction State Botanical Garden of South Carolina in 1992, which generated sufficient interest to implement plans for the conservatory.

FIG. 3–2 *Memorial Stadium Parking Lot*

The Columbia-based firm Boudreaux Hulstrand and Carter were selected as architects, assisted by Conklin Rossant Design of New York and Andropogon Associates, ecological planners and designers of Philadelphia.[24] Their breathtaking design in glass and polycarbonate steel featured all the elements that were included in the conceptual laundry list, notably a glass walkway called "walk among the treetops" which would have allowed visitors to look down on the vegetation (which included a collection of staghorn ferns) and cascading waterfall beneath.[25] The architectural drawings were completed in 1993 and publicized in issues of the *Botanical Garden Quarterly*, which listed the conservatory, with an associated amount of $4 million, as a naming opportunity until 1996. But when fundraising efforts failed to reach half of the projected cost, another garden project with different partners eclipsed the conservatory. That new partnership, formed with *Southern Living*, a lifestyle magazine based in Birmingham, Alabama, created home-landscaping plans using computer software.[26] By 1996 the partnership expanded to include others: the South Carolina Department of Parks, Recreation and Tourism; the city of Clemson; Duke Power; Metromont Materials Corporation; Vulcan Materials; Carolina Nurseries; and the South Carolina Heritage Corridor, which was a government initiative to link cultural historical and natural attractions on a 240-mile trail across fourteen counties. By late 1996 these partners embarked on a collaborative effort to create a "discovery center" (first called "the Wren House" and later the "Fran Hanson Discovery Center") and an adjacent natural history museum in the Botanical Garden as part of the Heritage Corridor.[27]

Although the garden conservatory failed to secure partnerships that generated adequate funding needed to succeed, the garden itself sparked initiatives. The recommendations of the Commission on the Future of Clemson University (CFC), a group of two hundred alumni and friends convened by President Deno Curris in 1995, corroborated the findings of Lennon's Second Century. The CFC found that developing creative partnerships at all levels within the University, and with off-campus constituencies, would address the challenges of an aging infrastructure and the reduction in state funding that began in the early 1990s.[28] The reduced state support coincided with the normal expected life span of many university facilities constructed in the 1950s.[29] To meet the challenges of new building construction, the CFC identified several areas in which new buildings would be needed[30] and recommended partnering with the corporate sector, alumni groups, healthcare providers, and business and industry leaders.[31]

FIG. 3-3

Botanical Garden
Conservatory

78

EUGENE MOORE DISCOVERY CENTER

FOR TEACHING AND LEARNING

1999

ONE PARTNERSHIP THAT originated from the CFC recommendations targeted improving education statewide through the rigorous training of educators. The Moore Discovery Center, which would have created a learning lab next door to the State Botanical Garden for use by students and teachers, grew from the report *Cutting Edge*, produced by the South Carolina Commission on Higher Education. The report was a plan to achieve academic excellence among higher education institutions in South Carolina; another, *Miles to Go South Carolina* from the Southern Education Foundation, was an apologia for the economic necessity of quality education.[32] The latter called education the "linchpin upon which future progress toward economic prosperity, development and a good quality of life rests" and revealed that in 1999 South Carolina ranked forty-first among the fifty states in terms of per capita personal income, with eighty-three percent of its residents having a high school education. South Carolina students lagged behind their peers in other states and placed in the bottom half of national rankings in terms of student test scores. Although high school graduation rates were near the national average, twenty-five percent of students in South Carolina schools with high levels of poverty were taught by teachers who lacked a major or minor in their field of instruction. The report criticized the practice of relying on "out of field" teachers, which further harmed low-performing schools with many needs, and termed the state of affairs as "a crisis in teacher preparation."[33]

Acting on the findings of these reports, the Clemson University School of Education proposed an education initiative to create a special center: a nationally recognized "incubator" to serve as a nexus for research and education, where discovery would drive the learning process. The creation of the "Eugene Moore Discovery Center for Teaching and Learning" sought to spark changes in teacher education structured around reformed and research-based teacher education programs; the center was to become the "leading change agent for education" in South Carolina "and beyond."[34] The School of Education and the Office for Development made the proposal to philanthropist Darla Moore, a native of Lake City, South Carolina, in honor of her father, Eugene T. Moore '49, who had committed his adult life to education as a teacher, coach, and principal in Florence County. Moore, herself a graduate of the University of South Carolina and George Washington University, had run Mesa, Inc., an ailing company involved in oil and gas production owned by magnate T. Boone Pickens, and brought it back to viability. Her business acumen and knowledge earned her acclaim in the media as "the Toughest Babe in Business."[35]

Moore's interest in education began, however, when she and her husband, Richard Rainwater, gave an initial contribution to the University of South Carolina's School of Business in 1998. At that time Moore researched the quality of education in South Carolina and the strength of the state's economy, which she described in this way: "to my horror, the results were just unacceptable. We simply had entirely too many students not performing at even basic levels, especially in poor and rural areas of the state."[36] Moore believed philanthropic acts would bring change, but only when performed with specific expectations:

Simply providing the political leaders with the results of world class, thoughtful research with recommended solutions did not lead to the transformational action that we wanted for the citizens of South Carolina. . . . I realized that for real metric-moving changes to occur, the private sector in local communities had to become the change agents for better education in their schools. . . . changes and innovation needed to improve student achievement would not be coming from the federal or state governments [and] private sector participation in public-private collaboration at the local level must be the catalyst for change.[37]

Moore Discovery Center

In its proposal, Clemson suggested for the Moore Discovery Center an eight-acre tract of land on the corner of Highway 76 and Silas Pearman Boulevard, adjacent to the State Botanical Garden. The site, once an orchard, had also been studied as a potential home for the visitor's center and an agricultural museum. The proximity of the Garden, with its nature trails, plants, pond life, and other natural features, along with the Campbell Geology Museum and Hanover House, afforded ideal opportunities for discovery and learning. The contemporary two-story brick building, as drawn in concept by Campus Planner Vander Mey, "harmonized with the Clemson University campus" and featured open and flexible internal spaces for research, presentations, exhibits, shops, and laboratories.[38] Although the School of Education, with the assistance of the Office for Development, introduced the initiative and crafted the proposal following a trend in transformative education at the time, the School and Moore never entirely embraced the Center concept.[39] Instead, in 2003 Moore and Rainwater directed their bequest to establish the Eugene T. Moore School of Education at Clemson, which is nationally renowned for its classroom and clinical training programs for pre-service teachers, professional mentoring of early-career teachers, and cutting-edge continuing education for in-service teachers.[40]

JAMES FRAZIER BARKER

"As an architect, I have great respect for the power of an idea," stated James F. Barker in his inaugural address as President of Clemson University in 2000, "and I've learned that the finest ideas come quickly in a flash of genius, yet they have the substance to transcend time and grow more compelling and engaging with time." Those words hold special relevance to projects both built and unbuilt; Barker's program of campus development, reminiscent of those of former Presidents Riggs and Edwards, resulted in ten major academic buildings, plus other structures, additions, and welcoming green spaces across campus. Those accomplishments stand with other impressive achievements of his administration, notably, the rise of Clemson's ranking among public universities, the increase of funding for research, and the capture of national championships in athletics.

The first architect to serve as President, Barker received his degrees from Clemson and Washington University in St. Louis. He began his career as a project designer for Stevens and Wilkinson (Atlanta, Georgia), then worked as associate designer for McCarty, Bullock, Church, Holesaple (Knoxville, Tennessee), and later partner, Barker and Ruth, and Principal (Starkville, Mississippi). A distinguished career in higher education followed at the University of Tennessee and at Mississippi State University, where he also served as Dean of the School of Architecture. In 1986 Barker assumed the position of Dean of the College of Architecture, Arts and Humanities at Clemson, a post he kept until becoming President in 1999.

In addition to the Moore Discovery Center, other partnerships related to campus development originated from CFC recommendations and findings. One concept introduced by the CFC, the "Clemson Experience," articulated ways to maximize the benefits of undergraduates' years spent at Clemson, and a specific recommendation to "maintain the natural beauty of the Clemson campus through carefully planned and controlled development."[41] That idea became a key component of the program of campus growth and development begun by President James F. Barker in 2000. A professional architect, Barker initiated the creation of a new master plan that reflected a fresh vision to guide long-range planning and physical development over eighteen years. The plan set the bar high: adding buildings totaling 1.5 million square feet, doubling the annual investment in facilities, and adopting guidelines to create a sustainable and environmentally responsible campus.[42] Published by Dober, Lidsky, Craig and Associates in three parts in 2002, followed by supplemental plans in 2003, 2004, and 2006, the plans called for new areas within precincts, green spaces, and development of the large underused open space south of Cooper Library.[43] The plan's *Summary Report* further articulated new thinking about campus development, envisioning the campus "as a garden—sacred ground where careful cultivation of the earth and cultivation of the mind come together to foster learning, creativity, collegiality and intellectual growth."[44] With the cooperation of numerous partners, that idea reshaped the campus over the next fifteen years, resulting in new green spaces and upwards of a dozen new structures.[45] Projects that did not come to fruition resulted when partnerships failed to coalesce, project timing did not synchronize with other institutional initiatives, or because unpredictable economic forces interceded; notwithstanding, THEY EMBODIED DILIGENT PLANNING, CREATIVITY, AND IMAGINATIVE THINKING.

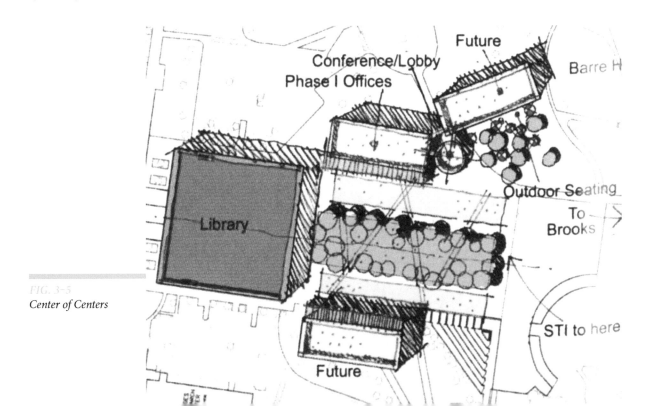

FIG. 3-5
Center of Centers

RESEARCH FACILITIES

COMMUNICATIONS CENTER

MIXED-USE / COMMERCIAL

RESIDENTIAL TOWNHOMES

OPEN SPACE

FORESTED LAND

MARINA

FIG. 3-6 *CURIOUS Campus, Aerial*

84

AMONG THE EFFORTS WITHIN the University to form partnerships that improved the teaching-learning experience, there were several individual initiatives. One such partnership focused on research, one of the pillars of Clemson's tripartite mission since the 1960s, but now with a new focus: research undertaken by undergraduates. A program initiated by Provost Doris Helms in 2003, Creative Inquiry, encouraged undergraduates to pursue research projects on their own that stimulated their intellectual curiosity, or to pair with others to investigate topics.

Acting on that idea, Professor of Civil Engineering Ben Sill and Professor of Landscape Architecture Dan Nadenicek, along with students Kathy Kuneyl, Richard Massingill, Kelly Miller, and Christopher Walsh in Nadenicek's studio class, developed the idea of the CURIOUS Campus: Clemson University Research Initiative Offered to Undergraduate Students. Sill and Nadenicek formulated the proposal on the premise that every student would derive benefits from a research experience in a living-learning environment on a campus devoted to creative inquiry. Philosophically, the concept embraced the Aristotelian view of *scholé*—connecting leisure with education, in which human activity and wellness are tied to learning and the sustainable use of the land. At Clemson, this was focused on the Experimental Forest.[46] The objectives were practical: to preserve and protect the Experimental Forest; assist economic development by connecting with industry, government, and entrepreneurship labs; and boost Clemson's position into the Top 20 tier of public institutions of higher education by attracting outstanding faculty and students. Prospective partners were to include the city of Clemson, Pickens and Oconee counties, local hospital systems, and Foothills YMCA.[47]

Described as a "village" built around a cluster of academic buildings and configured around a town center with planned green spaces and nature trails—a modern translation of basic ideas articulated by Frederick Law Olmsted a century before—CURIOUS Campus plans included classrooms, laboratories, studios, a library, a design cave, an auditorium, lecture halls, commercial spaces, restaurants, museums, and rental residences for "emeritus faculty of renown from around the globe," who would be housed in residences with access to Lake Hartwell.[48] Boat transport, or water taxis, would have shuttled students to the main campus and research sites of the Clemson Forest, Hopewell Plantation (the nineteenth-century home of former South Carolina Governor Andrew Pickens), Camp Hope, Musser Farm, the Eighteen Mile Creek wetlands, Martin Inn, Madren Center, and other locations. Every undergraduate student would use the campus to conduct projects and field experiments—plans projected as many as 14,000 students during the course of their Clemson careers, with 7,000 participating full time—mentored by as many as forty faculty members, creating "intergenerational mixing" and yielding a "community feel."[49]

SB 3-2 *Sill and Nadenicek*

CURIOUS

BENJAMIN SILL
AND
DANIEL NADENICEK

Sill and Nadenicek, both Clemson professors, developed the idea for CURIOUS campus in 2005 after reading the whitepaper "On Becoming Top-20 Clemson" by Provost Doris Helms. In that paper Helms wrote of the need to develop a strategy and a "big idea" that made Clemson unique and that would attract South Carolina's best students and the nation's most outstanding faculty. Clemson could not compete with other institutions by trying to be a "clone" of other Top 20 institutions, Helms believed, but would succeed by distinguishing its educational culture from all others.

That charge fueled Sill and Nadenicek to "think outside the box" to develop their CURIOUS Campus proposal; it postulated creative inquiry, research, and teamwork in the "CURIOUS Village," accessible by water taxi via Lake Hartwell, near the main campus of the University. The unlikely match of the two men also demonstrated untraditional thinking. Sill, a civil engineering professor, held an abiding love for the Clemson Experimental Forest and sustainability issues; he would later chair the President's Commission on Sustainability. Nadenicek, professor and chair of planning and landscape architecture, had focused his research on landscape history and architecture in nineteenth-century America, and introduced his students to the field in his design studios. Other University initiatives embraced the concept of undergraduate research, ultimately subsuming CURIOUS Campus, but the project embodied an idea and vision that grows more provocative with the passage of time as the shores of the Lake Hartwell reservoir continue to experience growing tourism and recreational development.

Sill and Nadenicek projected CURIOUS Campus on a thirty-acre site between Highway 93, Seneca Creek Road, and Lake Hartwell, commonly known as Y-Beach. They selected the site to take advantage of Lake Hartwell as a connection to other educational research sites, and because of its large open areas, beach access, and multiple lake inlets—a "modern image for a modern research campus."[50] Construction would have occurred in phases: first, a "core" consisting of a marina, restaurant, museum, and communication center, followed by other village buildings. The plan designated separate locations for research and enterprise initiatives (in the areas of advanced materials, technology-supported design, visualization, and educational cyber-infrastructure applications) and the environmental sciences (watersheds, forest resources, energy cycling, water quality, and lake biology). A gallery space for exhibiting and archiving Creative Inquiry products would have served as a major focal point.[51]

The cost, estimated at $25 million, and budget, prepared by the Spiro Center for Entrepreneurial Leadership, called for private financing from businesses, industries, endowments, and grants. Other sources of revenue would have included summer camp fees, paid by students of nearby colleges, program and event admission fees paid by students from public schools, parking fees for sporting and other university events, and the restaurant and daycare facility. Sill and Nadenicek envisioned CURIOUS Campus becoming part of the University's capital campaign and believed the project would be an "easy sell" compared with many of the other needs such as scholarships, academic space, and endowments that had high priority but lacked a "Wow!" factor.[52] They believed that donors who might not contribute to Clemson for those needs, would support the CURIOUS Campus. The timing of the project, however, did not synchronize with other ambitious university initiatives that were being planned or just getting started. The capital campaign, the Clemson University International Center for Automotive Research (CU-ICAR), the Urban Land Institute, and Creative Inquiry classes, which were growing in success and popularity, SUBSUMED THE CURIOUS CAMPUS.

COUNTESS ALICIA SPAULDING

PAOLOZZI BUILDING

2005, 2011

ANOTHER PROJECT, WHICH WAS similar to CURIOUS Campus, in that it embraced partnerships to maximize the Clemson experience for students, differed from others because it was planned for the city of Charleston and reflected Clemson's growing international outreach and focus. The Spaulding Paolozzi building, which might be viewed as a case study in the politics of modern urban design, represented an attempt to partner with a city government, a sister academic institution, and historic neighborhood associations to strengthen academic programs of the Clemson Architecture Center Charleston (CAC.C), located in the historic Cameron House on Bull Street. The CAC.C, established in 1988 as a collaborative effort of the College of Charleston and Clemson University, provided graduate-level instruction to architecture students.[53] Through the 1990s its directors, Ray Huff and Robert Miller, expanded the primary mission of the CAC.C to include the City of Charleston by offering assistance with design issues and planning advocacy. Increasing enrollments (and plans to quadruple the student body) necessitated a move to larger quarters on Franklin Street, the former Marine Hospital, in 1997.[54]

Continued growth brought with it a need for permanent space on George Street, across from Spoleto Festival headquarters.[55] A competition to design the new facility, named for Countess Alicia Spaulding Paolozzi, the co-founder of the Spoleto Festival in Italy and Charleston,[56] commenced in 2004. Forty applicants in five countries, with nine applicants from South Carolina, submitted designs.[57] The winner, W. G. Clark of Charlottesville, Virginia, whose firm had also won the design competition for the South Carolina

Aquarium, bowed out, and Kennedy & Violich Architecture (KVA) of Boston was awarded the commission.[58] KVA's design, produced by principals who specialized in green technology, Sheila Kennedy and Juan Frano Violich, featured a stucco and brick exterior and operable louvers to control the effects of the sun; a first-floor courtyard, shop, and gallery; second-floor studio space, a library, and seminar rooms; and additional studio space on the top story.

FIG. 3-8 *Spaulding Paolozzi, KVA*

FIG. 3-9 *Cloepfil*

The KVA design generated criticism from two local groups, the Preservation Society of Charleston and the Historic Ansonborough Neighborhood Association, who stated that the design did not fit and impacted the neighborhoods adversely.[59] Joined later by the Historic Charleston Foundation, the groups proposed as an alternative location Concord Park, a nine-acre development several miles south near the Cooper River, which was designated for a planned public park and was adjacent to the recently completed South Carolina Aquarium.[60] Charleston Mayor Joe Riley, however, favored the George Street location for the Center, saying that the proposed building would "fit well into the space" and would not "overwhelm 14 George Street or anything else."[61] President Barker also supported the location and design, and, in a commentary published in Charleston's *The Post and Courier*, welcomed public discourse on the project. He reaffirmed Clemson's commitment to public engagement throughout the Board of Architectural Review (BAR) hearing process[62] and reminded readers that Clemson representatives met with residents of Ansonborough and other community leaders and local groups to ensure that any building constructed was environmentally sensitive and technologically advanced.[63] In its articles and editorials *The Post and Courier* took the position that the Center was needed, but called on Clemson to "withdraw the plans and dramatically revise them."[64] The BAR voted six to one in favor of the design and granted conceptual approval for the building's proposed height, scale, and mass, but it did not grant final approval to proceed with construction.

To mitigate this setback, Clemson converted the George Street site into much-needed parking and purchased another lot, 292 Meeting Street, located in "a transitional zone having the commercial feel of Meeting Street and the residential feel of Ansonborough."[65] In late 2011, the Clemson Trustees approved plans to construct a new three-story, 31,000 square-foot Center on the site. This time, Allied Works Architecture of Portland, Oregon, led by Brad Cloepfil (also an entrant in the first competition), was chosen to design the new center because of the firm's experience in urban design, its commitment to sustainability, and its sensitivity to place and context.[66] Cloepfil's design featured classrooms, offices, studios, a library, a garden, and an exhibit space enclosed in a shell of glass, metal, and concrete, but the structure's most distinguishing exterior details—a curving white concrete wall and a four-inch thick aluminum screen with a series of holes—generated the most critical reaction.[67] Cloepfil, aware of the critical response, stated that he believed the resistance came because contemporary buildings did not have "detail and craft" and "a sense of being made," but that:

> Once people see things that are more responsive and thoughtful and particular to place, and hopefully beautiful, then people start to get attached to it. When you do contemporary work . . . people are nervous . . . but once it's built, they usually fall in love with it.[68]

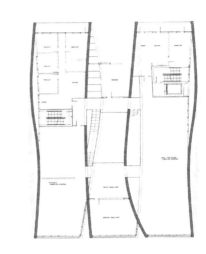
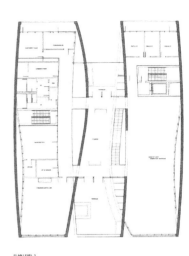

FIG. 3-10 *Spaulding Paolozzi Interior, Allied Works*

PLAN LEVEL 2

PLAN LEVEL 3

FIG. 3-11 *Spaulding Paolozzi Exterior, Allied Works*

93

In spite of pushback from community groups, the BAR granted conceptual approval for the design in October 2012 and preliminary approval in June 2014.[69] But in July, the Ansonborough and Charles Towne neighborhood associations, the Preservation Society, and the Historic Charleston Foundation filed suit in the Charleston County Court of Common Pleas, alleging that the BAR changed its rules after the design won conceptual approval.[70] According to the suit, the project was not "sympathetic to the historic feature that characterized its setting and context" and did not "adhere to, meet, or satisfy the Design Approval Standards."[71] The suit alleged that approval covered only the building's height, scale, and mass, but that, after the vote was taken, the BAR expanded conceptual approval to include "the general architectural direction and quality."[72] Calling the review process "flawed," the groups claimed that the plaintiffs and the public "were deprived of any meaningful opportunity to comment on the design of the project."[73] At a hearing before the BAR, residents spoke overwhelmingly against the project.

Faced with this opposition, in December 2014 Clemson University withdrew the Center application from consideration by the BAR and the action was dismissed.[74] Reiterating its commitment to "be a good neighbor and have a positive impact on the economy and quality of life in Charleston," Clemson announced plans to move the Center programs to the Cigar Factory on East Bay and Columbus streets.[75] This Victorian commercial structure, built in 1881, had operated as the Cotton Mill of Charleston and subsequently as a cigar factory, in 1912; it later achieved National Register status.[76] Carter Hudgins, director of Clemson's historic preservation program, summed up the Center's eight-year journey to its new home: "The Cigar Factory—as good an example as we have in Charleston for how a building almost given up for dead can be made profitable again—is an ideal location to teach the historical meaning of OLD BUILDINGS AND WHY THEY MATTER."[77]

CENTER FOR VISUAL ARTS

2006

JUST AS THE CURIOUS CAMPUS and the Spaulding Paolozzi building projects intended to maximize the Clemson experience for students, two additional contemporaneous projects embodied the concept in purpose, one in actual name. The Center for Visual Arts (2006) and the Clemson Experience (2008), developed within the course of two years, championed the Clemson experience and carried it forward. The Center for Visual Arts (CVA), called a "resource for artistic entrepreneurship with partners around the world,"[78] was born of a vision for the study of visual arts at Clemson University while providing the region with opportunities to explore creative processes. President Barker expressed the view that the CVA would "change both the perception and the reality of the Clemson Experience" for students and faculty and that the new facility would "bring the world to Clemson, and . . . Clemson to the world."[79] From its incipiency, the CVA planning committee envisioned the facility as transcending the boundaries of a conventional art museum, serving as a place where students, visitors, and scholars could engage directly in the creative process of artistic production by viewing, interpreting, and accessing "the artistic and cultural capital flowing through Clemson"—not solely in the visual arts, but also in other creative disciplines.[80]

FIG. 3-12
CVA, Aerial

In August 2007 the Campus Planning Office evaluated potential sites: one near the Strom Thurmond Institute and the Brooks Center; the area near Johnstone Hall and the central energy facility; the east and west sides of Cooper Library; a space between Mauldin and Long Halls; and an area adjacent to Edwards Hall. Each site offered advantages and disadvantages for pedestrian access, parking, access to utilities, and visibility. Of the six sites, the one near the Strom Thurmond Institute/Brooks Center offered the best accessibility to the public and students, as well as for service: the site progressed logically from the campus master plan, its strong spatial qualities offered the opportunity for a significant architectural presence, and the site had the potential to be linked to Lee Hall.[81] The location was situated directly in an area that campus planners referred to as the "green spine," a stretch of campus running from Bowman Field through the Carillon Garden, the Outdoor Theater, and the Reflection Pond to the lawn and valley of the Brooks Center, the Tiger Band practice fields, and into the valley beyond. The site also offered the potential to create a new southern, cross-campus pedestrian connection and feed into other established pedestrian paths, one being an informal path created by the Tiger Band from the Brooks Center through the woods to their practice field.[82] The site's adjacency to the Brooks Center afforded an opportunity to create a shared arts gateway and outdoor entry plaza with the CVA; such a gateway would enhance the arts experience for visitors upon arrival.[83]

The Boudreaux Group, an interdisciplinary design group based in Columbia, along with Smith Group in Washington DC and Seaman Whiteside Associates in Greenville, developed a conceptual design for use in fundraising. As the team began to develop the design concepts, four schemes emerged.[84] Each of the four addressed the site in different ways, with various relationships to the Brooks Center and the bridge using organizing elements such as an arts plaza, a garden or green space, a curve, and a courtyard.[85] When the design team presented its findings, it recommended the "Arts Plaza Scheme" which created the visual, not physical, effect of connecting the lobby of the Brooks Center for the Performing Arts with Lee Hall via a pedestrian bridge—in effect an arts gateway, with galleries visible to approaching pedestrians.[86]

Upon his review of the Arts Plaza Scheme, President Barker challenged the team to develop a fifth scheme, one he called "Building as Bridge" to express the vision of a building that physically spanned the ravine and connected Lee Hall with the Brooks Center. Barker had expressed his vision on such a structure as early as 2002 to architect Ben Rook:

> The idea of spanning the Campus Green with some form of a usable space has been the subject of several studies…This is one of the physical/conceptual connections that I would like to make on campus… The connection between Lee Hall and the Brooks Center needs to be one that is elegant and light: supportive to the idea of a continuous flow of east/west and north/south space. The Campus Green in a sense is the more significant and influential aspect of the planning concept. The idea of using the connection as a gallery space has a great deal of merit and the physical manifestation of this should be powerful and inspiring. Someone once commented on a work by Calatrava that "a sense of frozen movement is heightened by the lightness of the structure" [Barker's emphasis]. I'd like someone to make the same comment about the project that ultimately will make this connection at Clemson.[87]

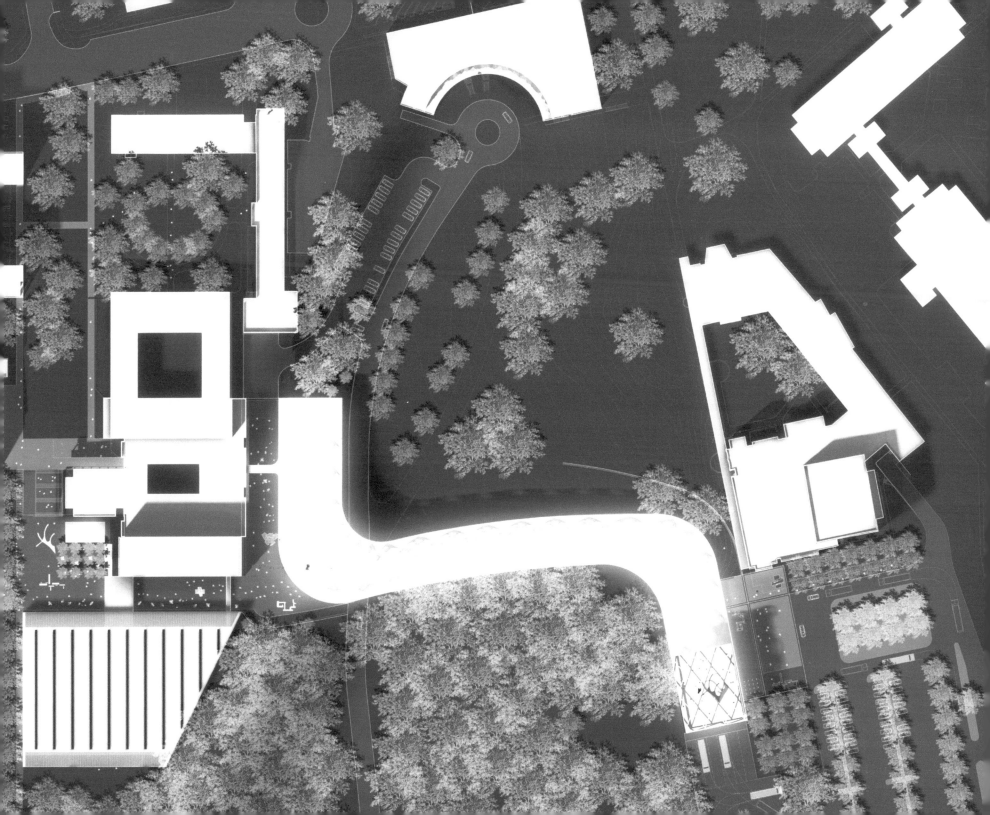

THOMAS PHIFER

"I arrived at Clemson in the early 1970s without a lot of confidence—extremely self-conscious, and not knowing how to make much of anything," Phifer said upon his induction into the College of Architecture, Arts and Humanities Hall of Fame in 2018. "The only thing I seemed to know how to do was to listen and emulate." Phifer credited his professors with developing his aptitudes and abilities: Joe Young with "learning to draw with precision and wonder"; Don Collins with "designing with geometric rigor"; John Jacques with "living life with unbridled joy"; and Wayne Drummond with "encouraging and supporting others." Phifer believed such examples impact teaching positively: "If we learn this way, we will teach this way."

Phifer's design of the proposed, and as yet unbuilt, Center for Visual Arts, exemplified modernism. The ethereal glass bridge, designed to span a lush ravine, physically and intellectually connected the Brooks Center for the Performing Arts with the expanded Lee Hall, better known as Lee III, which Phifer designed in 2011.

A native of Columbia, South Carolina, Phifer received his bachelor's and master's degrees from Clemson. He established his architecture firm in New York City in 1997 after working for modernist architect Richard Meier. Acclaimed as a "master of meticulous modernism," Phifer expresses his aesthetic in private homes as well as award-winning public buildings, such as the North Carolina Museum of Art (Raleigh) and Brochstein Pavilion (Houston), and has received numerous national and international prizes and awards.

Using the Building as Bridge scheme proposed by Barker, the design team developed four additional concepts.[88] The first formed around the idea of tension as a force acting through the bridge, and the relationships between form and structure as found in nature. The second scheme elevated the building upon stilts and made the least impact on the site. The third scheme employed a trestle or long-span truss bridge, with CVA functions spread along the bridge, producing a structure that yielded a glowing lantern effect at night. The fourth scheme, and the one preferred by the design team, employed the idea of a "path" to art from conception to exhibition. Beginning on the Lee Hall end of the bridge, one would first encounter faculty and student spaces where ideas were first conceptualized, then move on to the painting and drawing studios where art assumed material form. The bridge then culminated in a formal, abstract building, which housed galleries, classrooms, and other spaces for people to interact with art, people, and the community. A floating, modulating canopy connected the entire structure from Lee Hall to the gallery building, which was a five-story anchor to the bridge at the easternmost end, where it opened to the arts plaza and the Brooks Center.[89]

As the team discussed and debated the concepts, construction of an addition to Lee Hall (named Lee III) commenced and presented an opportunity for the architect of that project, Thomas Phifer, to produce yet another vision of the CVA. Phifer, who earned his architecture degrees from Clemson and had received the Medal of Honor from the American Institute of Architects in 2004, was invited by President Barker to produce his CVA design using the building-as-bridge concept. Phifer's space-age, futuristic design, one that curved across the ravine and linked Lee Hall with the Brooks Center, also housed sculpture, ceramics, photography, and printmaking studios, as well as administrative offices, a lecture hall, a gallery, and an outdoor sculpture area.[90] Discussions at the outset of the feasibility study in 2006 estimated construction costs in the range of $15 to $20 million, but that amount escalated when the team abandoned the first series of concepts and developed the building-as-bridge concepts. Using site photographs, topographic surveys, and program and project goals, Greenville's Aiken Cost Consultants developed a cost model of the final design that estimated construction in 2010 at $46 million, with a range as high as $70 million. To date, the Center for Visual Arts remains "a vision so compelling and imaginative that it will attract a donor UNLIKE ANY THAT CLEMSON HAS EVER SEEN."[91]

ALMOST AS SPECTACULAR as the Center for Visual Arts but planned for the northeast quadrant of campus, the Clemson Experience building debuted in concept in the campus master plan of 2002. Described at that time as "a new Clemson icon," the structure asserted itself as a one-stop shop for student services, such as admissions, registration, and financial aid, and was to be located near Clemson House across from the President's Park. Six years later, the idea was formally unveiled as a "bold idea to demonstrate the Clemson of tomorrow" and of "collaboration at its best, a showcase of campus planners, architects, designers, engineers, environmentalists, educators, and marketers."[92] Envisioned as a high-tech introduction to Clemson for visitors and prospective students while providing space for student activities, the Clemson Experience facility would have incorporated a visitor's center, admissions office, alumni affairs, public affairs, development, the Clemson Brand Center, broadcasting facilities, classrooms, meeting space, and retail space. Its 60,000–90,000 square-foot design would free approximately 45,000 square feet of administrative space in the central campus for academic uses. The new high-tech facility also afforded key space to other mission-essential functions which were then housed in the Alumni Center, Visitors Center, Shirley House, Littlejohn House, Trustee House, and Poole Hall.[93]

100

CLEMSON EXPERIENCE BUILDING
2008

FIG. 3-14 *Clemson Experience Buiding*

Planners first considered a site in the Douthit Hills reclamation area, but later rejected it as plans for student housing simultaneously progressed. The second projected location, near Clemson House and across from President's Park, became the final choice. The Pazdan-Smith Group (later McMillan Pazdan Smith) of Atlanta, Georgia produced the architectural drawing of the structure, certified by LEED (Leadership in Energy and Environmental Design), a rating system of the United States Green Building Council (USGBC), begun in 1998 for the design, construction, operation, and maintenance of environmentally sustainable buildings.[94] The five-story rectangular design, nestled among trees overlooking Bowman Field, featured a 6,000 square foot grand lobby, sheathed in glass.

FIG. 3-15 *Clemson Experience Building, Setting*

The building, estimated at a cost of $30–$40 million, was targeted for completion in 2010. The initial funding concepts called for the building to be owned by the Clemson University Foundation (CUF) on ground leased from the University, with the bulk of the funds raised from private sources.[95] Although the concept gained the approval of the CUF board, President Barker, the Vice-presidents, the Administrative Council, and the Board of Trustees, its path to completion collided with a period of general economic decline in world markets in what would later be called the Great Recession, beginning in December 2007. In the United States nine million jobs were lost in 2008–09, along with an estimated forty percent of the nation's gross domestic product.[96] In South Carolina, the recession doubled the number of unemployed and accelerated a shift in the state's economy from labor-intensive, lower-wage manufacturing to high-technology, better-paying employment.[97] In an attempt to alleviate the financial crisis, Clemson adopted a self-imposed building moratorium in fall 2008 to address the serious state funding crunch. In September 2010, the State Budget and Control Board voted to suspend capital projects at colleges that raised tuition costs seven percent or higher; those institutions affected included Clemson, the College of Charleston, the Medical University of South Carolina, and the Citadel.[98] With growing enrollment predicted and housing a pressing need the Douthit Hills project, with its 1,600-plus beds, mixed retail, and student amenities took priority over the Clemson Experience, which spelled its demise. Although the project did not come to fruition elements of the concept survived, however, in a new rendition called "EXPERIENCE CLEMSON," a state-of-the-art satellite center and interactive virtual museum, the brainchild of Neill Cameron, Vice-president of Institutional Advancement. It debuted in downtown Greenville September 2015.[99]

EPILOGUE

THE CLEMSON EXPERIENCE serves as but one example of how economic trends and conditions largely determined the outcomes of building projects throughout the history of Clemson University. Economic fluctuations, which produced growth and prosperity in one period and uncertainty and stagnation in another, challenged efforts to fulfill Clemson's institutional mission. Through no fault of the planners or the planning process, the effort to transform visions and plans into reality sometimes failed, as the twists and turns of events at home and abroad steered the construction of buildings and campus development. Although visionary partnerships helped leverage assets to make dollars stretch to obtain maximum gains, partnerships that failed to coalesce left some visions unrealized and buildings unbuilt. Those visions and plans that did not transform into reality may lead one to conclude they failed, or that they are dead. In actuality, they were only delayed, though sometimes the delay lasted a generation.[1]

Unbuilt, therefore, may not be as final as commonly believed. Rather than interpret the word as a judgment or a grim epitaph, one might apprehend its meaning more clearly as a holding pattern, or suspended progress. This pragmatic interpretation accommodates delays and other contingencies, and offers the thrilling prospect that so-called UNBUILT PROJECTS MAY ONE DAY BECOME A REALITY.[2]

ACKNOWLEDGMENTS

UNBUILT CLEMSON WOULD NOT HAVE BEEN POSSIBLE without the assistance, encouragement, and sage advice of colleagues, mentors, and friends. All deserve my heartfelt thanks and gratitude.

Many people facilitated this project and were critical to its success. Provost Robert H. Jones, acting on the recommendations of former Dean of Libraries Maggie Farrell and Library Chair Peggy Tyler, granted my request for the sabbatical leave that enabled me to undertake research and complete a first draft. Individuals at the Clemson University Press—Director John Morgenstern, Managing Editor Alison Mero, and graduate assistants Abby Maxim, who developed preliminary layouts, and Lindsay Scott, who designed the final graphics and page designs—supported the project from the beginning with guidance, counsel, and sustained interest. Others in my "library family" helped with the nitty-gritty of research. Kathy Edwards, librarian in the Gunnin Architecture Library, located relevant source material and sought additional funds to defray costs associated with publication; our field trips to neighboring institutions to study Bruce and Morgan buildings and our exploration of the Clemson campus on foot (in summer and winter) to experience its topography and layout, remain an indelible memory. Brenda Burk, Head of Special Collections and Archives, encouraged and supported my research, and retrieved large numbers of boxes; others there, James Cross, Susan Hiott, Breanna Johnson, Krista Oldham, Carl Redd, and Laurie Varenhorst, cheerfully located sources and materials during my weekly visits to the reading room. What true friends! Librarians in the R. M. Cooper Library also provided exemplary service: Suzanne Rook Schilf and Renna Redd delivered sources not available locally and on microfilm with incredible efficiency; Anne Grant helped interpret cryptic citations in online guides and indexes; and Digital Projects Manager Josh Morgan, along with Digital Lab Manager Darius Jones, scanned original documents to enhance their visual appeal. Thank you, all!

Information on several of the unbuilt projects came through interviews with key individuals at Clemson University. Campus Planner Gerald Vander Mey offered needed perspective on contemporary campus development and building construction; his personal remembrances, insights, and provision of source material helped tremendously. Vice-president for Public Service and Agriculture George Askew answered questions about the numerous farm and agricultural buildings that were constructed. Director of Historic Properties Will Hiott related facts about the relocation of Hanover House from the low country to campus and discussed the role of Rudolph Lee, whose many campus buildings stand as his enduring legacy. Professor of City Planning Clifford Ellis provided up-to-date information on campus planning and development. Lee Gallery Director Denise Woodward-Detrich also contributed information about the Center for Visual Arts.

Informal meetings and interviews with others formerly at Clemson University, but now retired, yielded a wealth of wisdom and offered leads to additional information. President Emeritus and architect James F. Barker and Provost Emerita Doris Helms offered constructive comments and provided context critical to understanding recent building projects and University initiatives. Jerome V. "Jerry" Reel, Professor Emeritus and former Clemson University Historian, sparked my interest in the subject of unbuilt architecture and the need to document such projects; his two-volume history of the University, *The High Seminary*, provided checks and balances to my interpretation of facts and served, I say with great relief, as a "safety net." Vice-president for Development Neill Cameron supplied several documents and spoke enthusiastically about the Clemson Experience and other notable projects underway at the time. Professor Emeritus Ben Sill, originator of CURIOUS Campus, answered countless questions and generously shared primary source material about that innovative project. Professors Emeriti John Jacques and Lynn Craig answered questions about contemporary campus planning history and provided documents. Director of University Relations Harry Durham clarified fundraising efforts for the Strom Thurmond Development project, and Ann Russell, independent scholar and biographer of Anna Calhoun Clemson, offered fascinating details on the Clemsons and their home, Fort Hill. Past Director of the Clemson Botanical Garden David Bradshaw recounted the historical development of the South Carolina State Botanical Garden, and John Bodiford, senior horticulturist, led me on an enlightening tour of various sites within the Garden. Librarian Emerita Gail Julian served as a sounding board for all sorts of questions, offered needed objectivity, and boosted me when I most needed it.

Librarians and archivists elsewhere proved instrumental in obtaining other primary textual sources. Three people at Winthrop University (the once all-female counterpart to the then all-male Clemson College)—Director of Special Collections Gina Price White, Vice-president for Facilities Management Walter Hardin, and Research Director in Advancement Services Jane Starnes— arranged tours of Winthrop's three Bruce and Morgan buildings on a scorching day in July. In Atlanta, Jody Thompson (Georgia Tech) and Marianne Bradley (Agnes Scott College) provided campus plans and building data on the Bruce and Morgan buildings on those campuses. For information on campus planners Perry, Shaw and Hepburn, Kehoe and Dean, Jeffrey Makala (Furman University) provided original correspondence between Furman officials and the architects, and Marianne Martin (Rockefeller Library, Colonial

Williamsburg Foundation, which holds the papers of William Graves Perry) graciously assisted me during and after my visit there.

Special thanks go to those who furnished photographs: Stuart Ferguson, archivist at the Highlands Historical Society in North Carolina; Britt Ambruson, marketing coordinator at Perry Dean Rogers in Boston, successors to the firm of Perry, Shaw and Hepburn, Kehoe and Dean; Sheila Kennedy, principal, and Karaghen Hudson, studio manager, at Kennedy & Violich Architects, Boston; Ken Robertson of Thomas Phifer and Partners, New York; Brittany Vega, Studio Assistant, at Allied Works, Portland, and Kim Poole of Craig Gaulden Davis in Greenville. A poignant thank you, in memoriam, goes to architect Charles Lyman Bates '53 (and his children, Jamie and Charles, for their assistance). Soon after reviewing the section about the Multi-purpose Auditorium and granting me an interview to learn about the project, the elder Mr. Bates passed away; however, his life and prolific accomplishments remain as testament to his design aesthetic.

FINALLY, TO THOSE WHO UNDOUBTEDLY HELPED, BUT WHOSE NAMES I FAILED TO WRITE DOWN OR REMEMBER, MY APOLOGIES BUT SINCERE THANKS.

D. S. TAYLOR

SEPTEMBER 2020

NOTES

FOREWORD

1 The *Long-Range Framework Plan* is a decision-making tool. It charts an overall structure for future development, new open spaces, and mobility networks, while allowing flexibility to enable the University to respond to changing conditions and circumstances. *Clemson University Long-Range Framework Plan* (Clemson, SC: Clemson University, 2017), https://cufacilities.sites.clemson.edu/documents/planning/LRFP_lowres.pdf.

INTRODUCTION

1 Daniel M. Abramson, "Stakes of the Unbuilt," The Aggregate, February 2, 2014, http://we-aggregate.org/piece/stakes-of-the-unbuilt.

2 Abramson, "Stakes of the Unbuilt"; Anupriya Saraswat, "Unbuilt Architecture—Unbuilt Seeks to Celebrate Not Only What Could Have Been, But Also What We Will Leave Behind," ArchitectureLive!, accessed March 3, 2020, https://architecturelive.in/unbuilt-architecture-unbuilt-seeks-to-celebrate-not-only-what-could-have-been-but-also-what-we-will-leave-behind/.

3 Linda Besner, "Once in a Blue Moon: What We Can Learn from Things That Never Happened," *Globe and Mail* (Toronto, ON), August 9, 2019, https://www.theglobeandmail.com/opinion/article-once-in-a-blue-moon-what-we-can-learn-from-things-that-never-happened/.

4 Quoted in Niall Ferguson, ed., *Virtual History: Alternatives and Counterfactuals* (New York: Basic Books, 1999), 7.

CHAPTER ONE

1 *Annual Report of the Trustees of the Clemson Agricultural College to the General Assembly of South Carolina* (Columbia, SC: State Printer, October 1890), n.p. The Trustees specified these buildings: Main Building with an attached chapel, three dormitories, a mess hall, a mechanical hall, ten houses for professors, a hospital, a creamery, and barns for livestock.

2 *Annual Report of the Trustees of the Clemson Agricultural College to the General Assembly of South Carolina* (Columbia, SC: State Printer, October 1890), n.p.; Richard D. Funderburke,"Bruce and Morgan," New Georgia Encyclopedia, Dec. 7, 2016, https://www.georgiaencyclopedia.org/articles/arts-culture/bruce-and-morgan. Bruce and Morgan were renowned for their academic buildings, courthouses, opera houses, and libraries in the southeastern United States. Their designs combined elements of Romanesque Revival, Queen Anne, Second Empire, and Gothic Revival, featuring arches, bracketed eaves, terra cotta embellishments, and classical symmetry. In South Carolina, Bruce and Morgan designed main buildings at Converse College in Spartanburg (1890) and the Winthrop Normal and Industrial College at Rock Hill (1895).

3 *Annual Report of the Trustees*, 1890, n.p. The Trustees first offered the presidency to Stephen D. Lee, President of the Agricultural and Mechanical College of Mississippi, but he declined.

4 Jerome V. Reel, *The High Seminary* (hereinafter *THS*), vol. 1 (Clemson, SC: Clemson University Digital Press, 2011), 80. A Bruce and Morgan representative also returned to campus in May 1894 after the Main Building burned to supervise rebuilding.

5 CULSC&A, MSS 96, f 14, Richard Wright Simpson Papers, Letters of Henry A. Strode, November 1890–December 1890.

6   CULSC&A, MSS 96, Henry A. Strode to Richard Wright Simpson, November 5, 1890. Simpson wrote that the Trustees "resolved the location," but he did not divulge if the Trustees arrived at the decision independently, or based their decision upon the wishes of Thomas and Anna, as some sources indicate, or if Anna alone selected the site, as local legend has it. See Clemson University College of Architecture, Arts and Humanities (hereafter CAAH), Department of Planning and Landscape Architecture, *Campus Preservation and Clemson Historic Resources: Seminar Proceedings*, (Clemson, SC: Clemson University, 1995), 39–41; Wright Bryan, *Clemson: An Informal History of the University, 1889–1979* (Columbia, SC: R. L. Bryan Co.), 34. In either instance, the location respected the both the traditional entry drive to Fort Hill (today located in front of Sikes Hall) and the parade ground (Bowman Field), which was used for mandatory military training as stipulated in the Morrill Act. The parade ground served as a key organizing element in the original campus.

7   CAAH, *Campus Preservation*, 41.

8   *Report of the Trustees of the Clemson Agricultural College* (Columbia, SC: State Printer, October 1891) n. p.

9   Reel, *THS*, vol. 1, 153, 162.

10   Paul V. Turner, *Campus: An American Tradition* (Cambridge, MA: MIT Press, 1984), 158. Baseball was first played at Clemson in April 1896; football followed in the autumn of that year. Although some institutions had begun in the 1850s to include athletics as part of the educational experience, most colleges did not host athletic competitions between institutions until the 1860s; at that time gymnasia afforded a new venue for some competitive sports. By the late nineteenth century, collegiate athletics were well organized nationwide and had become an integral part of modern college life.

11   "Annual Report of the President of the College, November 24, 1900," in *Eleventh Annual Report of the Board of Trustees of Clemson Agricultural College, 1900*, (Columbia, SC: State Printers, 1901), 16.

12   "Report of the Board of Visitors to the Board of Trustees of Clemson Agricultural College," April 17, 1903, in CULSC&A, S 30, Minutes, 1903.

13   Reel, *THS*, vol. 1, 162, 250.

14   Reel, *THS*, vol. 1, 72–73.

15   See *Annual Report of the Trustees to the General Assembly of South Carolina* (Columbia, SC: State Printer, 1890–1910). Although extant records of this period contain no campus planning documents as such, information about building construction, as well as efforts to develop portions of the campus, may be gleaned from archival records.

16   *Acts and Joint Resolutions of the General Assembly of the State of South Carolina* (Columbia, SC: State Printer 1900), 565, accessed via https://babel.hathitrust.org. The act also permitted the construction of other roads and tramways within its incorporated limits. Details of the original request to construct the rail line are found in the *Tenth Annual Report of the Board of Trustees of Clemson Agricultural College, 1899* (Columbia, SC: Bryan Printing Co., 1900), 7. For additional details, see also CULSC&A, S 30, Minutes, August, 8, 1899.

17   CULSC&A, S 30, Minutes, March 20, 1900.

18   CULSC&A, S 30, Minutes, February 27, 1900, March 20, 1900, March 8, 1901.

19   CULSC&A, S 30, Minutes, May 29, 1903.

20   CULSC&A, S 18, f 69, Report "Electric Road to Calhoun," March 6, 1909.

21   CULSC&A, S 18, f 9, Patrick H. Mell to John Wannamaker, June 8, 1904.

22   Todd Jones, "A History of Keney Park," (unpublished manuscript, 2011), 16–17, https://www.gchartford.org/keney_park/History%20of%20Keney%20Park.pdf; "George Parker Dead," *New York Times*, September 14, 1926, 29. Hartford enjoyed a reputation as "America's Park City" for its lush parks, many of which were created by Frederick Law Olmsted and the Olmsted Brothers.

23   CULSC&A, S 18, f 10, Patrick H. Mell to John Wannamaker, July 7, 1904. The author found no record to confirm that Parker delivered a lecture. The Farmer's Institute was an annual meeting of farmers to meet and share agricultural information and farming methods, and was held on Bowman Field.

24   CULSC&A, S 18, f 25, Benjamin Tillman to Patrick H. Mell, December 8, 1905; Patrick H. Mell to George Parker, December 6, 1905. The plans Parker created are not found in either the records of the Clemson Board of Trustees or in the records of President Mell.

25   CULSC&A, S 18, f 25, George Parker to Patrick H. Mell, December 4, 1905, December 9, 1905.

26   Loren M. Wood, *Beautiful Land of the Sky: John Muir's Forgotten Eastern Counterpart, Harlan P. Kelsey, Pioneering Our Native Plants and Eastern National Parks* (Bloomington: iUniverse, 2013), 100–02.

27   Wood, *Beautiful Land of the Sky*, 117–20.

28   Daniel Vivian, "Kelsey and Guild," in *South Carolina Encyclopedia* (Columbia, SC: University of South Carolina Press, 2006), 515–

16; Marta Leslie Thacker, "Working for the City Beautiful: Civic Improvement in Three South Carolina Communities" (unpublished MA thesis, University of South Carolina, 1999). Monaghan Mills was later sold to J.P. Stevens and Co. In 2006 the building and property became The Lofts of Greenville.

29   "Work for the Women," *The State* (Columbia, SC), January 28, 1904, 2; untitled article, *The State*, January 29, 1904, 8; "Society in South Carolina," *News and Courier* (Charleston, SC), January 31, 1904, 10.

30   "Work for the Women," *The State* (Columbia, SC), January 28, 1904, 2; untitled article, *The State*, January 29, 1904, 8; "Society in South Carolina," *News and Courier* (Charleston, SC), January 31, 1904, 10; Vivian, "Kelsey and Guild," 515–516. See also, Kelsey and Guild Landscape Architects, *Beautifying and Improving Greenville, South Carolina: Report to the Municipal League of Greenville, South Carolina* (Boston, MA: Kelsey and Guild, 1907).

31   CULSC&A, S 18, f 25, Benjamin Tillman to Patrick H. Mell, December 8, 1905. These plans do not exist today.

32   CULSC&A, S 18, f 28, Patrick H. Mell to Harlan P. Kelsey, March 5, 1906.

33   CULSC&A, S 18, f 28, Harlan P. Kelsey to Patrick H. Mell, March 12, 1906.

34   CULSC&A, S 18, f 28, Patrick H. Mell to Harlan P. Kelsey, March 14, 1906.

35   CULSC&A, S 18, f 54, Patrick H. Mell to Harlan P. Kelsey, October 14, 1907.

36   CULSC&A, S 18, f 55, Harlan P. Kelsey to Patrick H. Mell,

October 19, 1907.

37 CULSC&A, S 18, f 58, Harlan P. Kelsey to Patrick H. Mell, December 31, 1907. The Hotel was demolished in 1950.

38 CULSC&A, S 18, f 58, Patrick H. Mell to John Wannamaker, December 17, 1907.

39 CULSC&A, S 18, f 58, Patrick H. Mell to John Wannamaker, December 17, 1907.

40 CULSC&A, S18, f 59, Patrick H. Mell to John Wannamaker, January 29, 1908. Mell cited excerpts of Tillman's letter. Tillman was referring to Prosper Jules Berckmans, a Belgian horticulturist and owner of Fruitland Nursery in Augusta, GA. After the nursery was sold in 1931 it became home to the Augusta National Golf Course.

41 CULSC&A, S 18, f 60, Patrick H. Mell to George Parker, February 3, 1908.

42 CULSC&A, S 18, f 60, George Parker to Patrick H. Mell, February 5, 1908.

43 CULSC&A, S 18, f 63–64, John Wannamaker to Patrick H. Mell, April 1, 1908, May 2, 1908.

44 CULSC&A, S 18, f 66, Patrick H. Mell to John Wannamaker, July 1, 1908. Mell recapped the events of the preceding months.

45 CULSC&A, S 18, f 64–65, Patrick H. Mell to John Wannamaker, May 30, 1908, June 10, 1908.

46 Wood, *Beautiful Land*, 100–02.

47 Commissioner of Agriculture, Commerce and Industries of the State of South Carolina, *Ninth Annual Report*, (Columbia, SC: Gonzales and Bryan, State Printers, 1912), 110.

48 Walter Riggs, "Clemson College in 1924," *The Tiger*, March 12, 1914, 2–4.

49 Walter Riggs, "Clemson College in 1924," *The Tiger*, March 12, 1914, 2–4.

50 Walter Riggs, "Clemson College in 1924," *The Tiger*, March 12, 1914, 2–4.

51 "Memorial to Walter Merritt Riggs, President of the Clemson Agricultural College," April 16, 1926, 36.

52 CULSC&A, S 30, *[President's] Report to the Board of Trustees*, July 2, 1918, 1.

53 Donald M. McKale and Jerome V. Reel, Jr., eds., *Tradition: A History of the Presidency of Clemson University* (Macon, GA: Mercer University Press, 1988), 101.

54 CULSC&A, S 30, *President's Annual Report to the Board of Trustees*, March 6, 1911, 32.

55 CAAH, *Campus Preservation*, 1995, 45.

56 Alan Schaffer, *Visions. Clemson's Yesteryears, 1880s–1960s* (Louisville, KY: Harmony House, 1960), 24.

57 CULSC&A, S 30, *President's Report to the Board of Trustees*, July 11, 1911, 2; July 9, 1912, 14. Plans for the pavilion do not exist.

58 CULSC&A, S 30, *President's Report to the Board of Trustees*, July 11, 1911, 2; July 9, 1912, 14; Walter Riggs, "Clemson College in 1924," *The Tiger*, March 12, 1914, 2–4.

59 CULSC&A, S 30, *President's Report to the Board of Trustees*, July

9, 1912, 14.

60   CULSC&A, S 30, *President's Report to the Board of Trustees*, December 1, 1920, 32–33.

61   CULSC&A, S 30, *President's Report to the Board of Trustees*, November 4, 1922, 24.

62   CULSC&A, S 30, *President's Report to the Board of Trustees*, June 15, 1934, 18.

63   CULSC&A, S 30, *President's Report to the Board of Trustees*, June 15, 1934, 18; Reel, *THS*, vol. 1, 240–41; McKale and Reel, *Tradition*, 157.

64   CULSC&A, S 30, *President's Report to the Board of Trustees*, June 15, 1934, 18–19. After the Agricultural Hall was destroyed by fire in 1925, officials decided that it should be rebuilt as a library and that a new agriculture building was needed.

65   Reel, *THS*, vol. 1, 250.

66   The buildings constructed were the Bowen, Bradley, Donaldson, Wannamaker, and Norris dormitories, Long Hall, and Sirrine Hall.

67   Reel, *THS*, vol. 1, 255–56; "Clemson Experimental Forest," Wikipedia, accessed Sep. 29, 2016, https://en.wikipedia.org/wiki/Clemson_Experimental_Forest. Starting in 1933, the federal government began to purchase land, which was low in productivity because of drought and improper farming, as part of its Land Utilization Program. By 1935 the program, through a series of requests by Clemson officials, transferred more than 27,000 acres of land located in Pickens and Anderson counties to the care of Clemson College. This major land acquisition, most of which became the Clemson Experimental Forest, would later serve to promote Clemson's education and public service missions and foster the development of curricula and degree programs in agriculture and forestry, which relied on the forest for lab assignments and fieldwork.

68   CULSC&A, S 30, *President's Report to the Board of Trustees*, June 18–19, 1937.

69   CULSC&A, S 30, *President's Report to the Board of Trustees*, October 1939, 2.

70   Sikes wrote: "Those in authority have from time to time stressed the necessity of planning for the future. The records reveal the fact that in 1914 and again in 1922 the Trustees made and revised plans for future growth and activities." *President's Report to the Board of Trustees*, June 17, 1938, 3. A search for these earlier reports turned up nothing. However, J. C. Littlejohn mentioned them in a letter to Lawrence Pinckney, State Administrator of the WPA, in March 1938: "The records of the College indicate that a rather comprehensive plan for growth of Clemson Agricultural College was made up by the Trustees in 1922. This plan was based on a report made in 1914 [probably that of President Riggs]. Due to lack of funds only a small beginning could be made in carrying out the long-range plans for the future development of Clemson College." Littlejohn listed eight projects that were completed with funds from the federal government and alumni. CULSC&A, S 2, f 7.

71   Reel, *THS*, vol. 1, 285.

72   CULSC&A, S 7, f 7–10, 1941–55. The files document the scope of activities.

73   One such reply, from Dean of the School of Chemistry and Geology, Dr. F. H. H. Calhoun, deserves note: "I do not see how the campus could be improved. It is so beautiful now it really hurts. I

think our main problem is to sell the beauty to students and have them feel about it the same as the rest of us do. Of course, new roads, new walks, and the adequate care of the grounds will make some improvements, but the fundamental things have been done already." CULSC&A, S 30, *President's Report to the Board of Trustees*, June 16, 1944, 6. In addition to the deans, engineer and alumnus F. R. R. Sweeny, who assessed the capacity and condition of college facilities, recommended further actions in a multipage report that was, in essence, a precursor to the first campus master plan. Sweeny wrote Superintendent of Grounds David Watson: "I was very much impressed by the fact that Clemson has set up a planning committee for future development on campus and that you were chairman of that committee." CULSC&A, S 7, Minutes, July 27, 1942.

74   The Cowling Arboretum at Carleton College in Northfield, Minnesota, 1920s; the Morris Arboretum at the University of Pennsylvania, 1932; and the University of Wisconsin-Madison Arboretum in 1934, successfully integrated arboreta with their missions.

75   CULSC&A, S 7, f 5.

76   CULSC&A, S 7, f 5, Minutes, March 24, 1944.

77   CULSC&A, S 7, f 7, "The Clemson Arboretum," February 20, 1948; David Watson to Robert Franklin Poole, March 8, 1948.

78   CULSC&A, S 18, f 28, Patrick H. Mell to Harlan P. Kelsey, March 13, 1906.

79   CULSC&A, S 18, f 29, Harlan P. Kelsey to Patrick H. Mell, March 26, 1906; McKale, *Tradition*, 80–81.

80   CULSC&A, S 18, f 55, Harlan P. Kelsey to Patrick H. Mell, October 19, 1907.

81   CULSC&A, S 30, Minutes, April 11–12, 1941, 277.

82   CULSC&A, S 30, Minutes, April 11–12, 1941, 277.

83   CULSC&A, S 7, f 7, "The Clemson Arboretum," February 20, 1948; David Watson to Robert Franklin Poole, March 8, 1948.

84   CULSC&A, S 7, f 7, David Watson to Robert Franklin Poole, October 25, 1948.

85   CULSC&A, S7, f 7, David Watson to J. C. Littlejohn, January 28, 1949.

86   "Clemson College Little Theater by Class 1916," *The Tiger*, May 17, 1941, 10.

87   "Clemson College Little Theater by Class 1916," *The Tiger*, May 17, 1941, 10; "Clemson Class of '16 to Give College $10,000 Little Theater," *Independent* (Anderson, SC), May 9, 1941, 14; "$10,000 Gift Be Presented Soon" [sic], *Independent*, May 19, 1941, 8.

88   CULSC&A, S 30, Minutes, June 15, 1951, 205.

89   CULSC&A, S 7, f 9, Minutes, July 2, 1951.

90   Alan Cannon, "Little Theatre Playhouse Renovation Begins Here," *The Tiger*, October 4, 1951, 6.

91   CULSC&A, S 11, f 433; S 30, Minutes, October 13, 1953, 344.

92   CULSC&A, "The Plan" (1953), in *Clemson College: Its Past and Future*, [1954].

93   CULSC&A, S 11, f 433, Harlan E. McClure to Robert Franklin Poole, April 6, 1956.

94   CULSC&A, S 30, Minutes, April 9, 1956, 496.

95   CULSC&A, S30, *Periodic Reports to the Board of Trustees*, May 29, 1957, 10.

96   "Hanover House (Clemson)," Wikipedia, accessed April 23, 2019, https://en.wikipedia.org/wiki/Hanover_House_(Clemson); Reel, *THS*, vol. 1, 335–36.

97   CULSC&A, S 87, b 15, f 13, David J. Watson, "Colonial Restoration," November 12, 1952.

98   Reel, *THS*, vol. 1, 335.

99   CULSC&A, S 7, f 5, J. C. Littlejohn to Robert Franklin Poole, August 21, 1941.

100   Reel, *THS*, vol. 1, 336.

101   CULSC&A, S 7, f 5, "Report of the Buildings and Grounds Committee," August 21, 1941.

102   CULSC&A, S 30, *President's Report to the Board of Trustees*, October 31, 1941, 36.

103   CULSC&A, S 30, Minutes, June 28, 1946, 601.

104   CULSC&A, S 7, f 9. Lee's actions at this time were later recorded in the Buildings and Grounds Committee Minutes.

105   CULSC&A, S 7, f 7, David Watson to Robert Franklin Poole, March 8, 1948. President Poole's handwritten message at the top of the letter reads "Keep for Board recommendation."

106   CULSC&A, S 7, f 9, Minutes, March 23, 1953; David Watson to Robert Franklin Poole, March 2, 1953. In 1953 the Class of 1915, whose President was Watson, purchased the house for $35 and moved it from its original site in Seneca, SC to campus. The house, built ca. 1825, was owned by the Hunt family. "Historic Old House Is Reconstructed," *Greenville News* (Greenville, SC), March 6, 1953, 34; Carol Anderson, "Log House on Campus Was Once Lodging Place for Travelers," *Messenger* (Clemson, SC), August 31, 1967, 17.

107   David Watson to Robert Franklin Poole, March 2, 1953; "Historic Old House Is Reconstructed," *Greenville News* (Greenville, SC), March 6, 1953, 34.

108   CULSC&A, S 7, f 9, Minutes, January 13, 1955.

109   See the present-day campuses of Lindenwood University, Defiance, MO, home of Boonesfield Village, and Wake Forest College, Winston-Salem, NC, home of Old Salem Village, for comparisons.

110   CULSC&A, MSS 41, a 97-14, Rudolph E. Lee Papers. One such structure was the residence of Professor J. H. Marshall.

111   "New Chemistry Building," *The Tiger*, March 2, 1945, 1. A search for these plans failed to locate them.

112   CULSC&A, S 7, f 9. "Annual Report of the Buildings and Grounds Committee," 1952–53. The report concluded "This Committee has considered very conscientiously all of the projects that came before it within the scope of its activity."

113   Perry, Shaw and Hepburn, Kehoe and Dean (PSHKD), "Birdseye View of Campus," *Clemson College Campus Master Plan*, 1954.

114   Since Lee did not include drawings for this "antebellum house" in his plans for the restoration area, and because his personal papers yield no clues as to his thoughts about it, one is left to surmise what he envisioned. In the strict sense of the word, "antebellum" meant a structure constructed or existing from the period after the

Revolutionary War and before the American Civil War. Antebellum architecture is characterized by Greek Revival, Georgian, and Neoclassical styles.

115   CULSC&A, S 7, f 5, David Watson to Robert Franklin Poole, April 4, 1945.

116   CULSC&A, S7, f 5, Robert Franklin Poole to David Watson, April 10, 1945.

117   Reel, *THS*, vol. 1, 444–45.

118   CULSC&A, S 7, Minutes, September 18, 1944.

119   The records do not indicate whether students were used in these projects, however.

120   CULSC&A, S 7, Minutes, November 9, 1944.

121   CULSC&A, S 30, *President's Report to the Board of Trustees*, June 15, 1945, 34. Ironically, in the same report Poole wrote that there had been "too much wasted effort in planning. It will be necessary for us to re-kindle a progressive, pioneering atmosphere."

122   CULSC&A, S 30, *President's Report to the Board of Trustees*, October 28, 1946, 12.

123   CULSC&A, S 30, *President's Report to the Board of Trustees*, October 28, 1946, 12. In September the Executive Committee of the Board of Trustees filed a postwar building program with the Federal Works Agency through the South Carolina Research, Planning and Development Board. The proposed projects included, first, a heating plant, followed by buildings for chemistry and engineering, dormitories, and a laundry.

124   CULSC&A, S 30, *President's Report to the Board of Trustees*,

October 28, 1946, 20. For the 1946–47 academic year, 2,964 students attended, compared to 752 in 1943–44.

125   Turner, *Campus: an American Tradition*, 267.

126   CULSC&A, S 30, *President's Report to the Board of Trustees*, October 28, 1946, 20. See photos depicting students parking their cars in contemporary editions of *Taps* and in the photographic collections of the Clemson University Archives.

127   CULSC&A, S 30, *President's Report to the Board of Trustees*, June 1949, 9.

128   Reel, *THS*, vol. 1, 325–37; "How Clemson Houses Veterans" (1948) in CULSC&A, S 37, f "Buildings—Publications." By the early 1980s these "prefabs" were being dismantled, moved elsewhere, or, according to Gary Gaulin, associate director of University Housing and Dining, used for training exercises for firefighters.

129   CULSC&A, S 30, Minutes, October 26, 1948, 789. John Gates also presented the Trustees with his plans for the development of housing projects, but the Board took no action on that plan.

CHAPTER TWO

1   "Historical Enrollment at a Glance (1900–2010)," Clemson University, accessed April 30, 2020, https://www.clemson.edu/institutional-effectiveness/documents/oir/historical/Historical-Enrollment-Detail.pdf. Women were first admitted as regular students in October 1954, ending the all-male military tradition. Other milestones occurred in January 1963 with the admission of African American Harvey Gantt to the architecture program, and in

July 1964 when the Clemson Agricultural College of South Carolina became Clemson University.

2   CULSC&A, S 30, *President's Report to the Board of Trustees*, October 26, 1948, 11. The plan created in 1945 was actually a campus atlas created by faculty of the Department of Civil Engineering. In 1944 the secretary of the State Sinking Fund Commission (the body which drew up Clemson's insurance policies) requested a map of the college showing the locations of buildings, water mains, roads, and other pertinent information. Initially, the Trustees appropriated $6,830 to create the map, but as time passed they spent almost $18,000 on its creation. "Map is prepared by Petroff and Gates," *The Tiger*, November 18, 1948, 2; CULSC&A, S 30, *President's Report to the Board of Trustees*, June 15, 1945, 29.

3   "Studies Clemson Master Building Plan," *Greenville News*, November 19, 1948, 1A.

4   For details on the controversy surrounding the building of the Hartwell Dam and the creation of Lake Hartwell, see Reel, *THS*, vol. 1, 431–35; CULSC&A, S 30, "Chronology of Hartwell Dam Project, 1949–1956," report prepared for the Board of Trustees of Clemson College, n.d.

5   "Clemson Studies on Dam Damage Is Pushed," *Greenville News*, April 29, 1961, 1D.

6   Mary Lou Culbertson, "Pressing Needs at Clemson Now Are Told Visiting Legislators," *Independent* (Anderson, SC), March 14, 1952, 1.

7   CULSC&A, S 30, *President's Report to the Board of Trustees*, October 20, 1952, 8.

8   CULSC&A, S 87, b 47, f 12, Memorandum of J. C. Littlejohn, February 10, 1954; CULSC&A, S 87, b 87, f 52, Vice-president for

Business and Finance records; these contain the contract between Clemson and architects PSHKD.

9   *Clemson College: Its Past and Future*, 9–11; Richard Dober, *Campus Planning* (New York: Reinhold, 1963), 4–72, provides an explanation of the types of campus planning.

10   Debbie Graham, "Evolutionary Process Serves Clemson's Growing Needs," *The Tiger*, November 2, 1973, 10–11; Dober, *Campus Planning*, 40, 213.

11   *Clemson College: Its Past and Future*, 10–11. See also the inside front cover, displaying an illustration of Fort Hill with this statement: "This beautiful old mansion *stands in the center of the College campus* [author's emphasis] and is open to the public."

12   "Proposed Scheme for the Development of Clemson Agricultural College," November 17, 1952, in drawings from PSHKD, *Clemson College: Its Past and Future*, 10–11.

13   "Proposed Scheme for the Development of Clemson Agricultural College," November 17, 1952.

14   CULSC&A, MSS 339, b 21, f 19, H. E. Glenn to Thomas Shaw, September 14, 1953; CULSC&A, S30, *President's Report to the Board of Trustees*, March 20, 1953, 17.

15   CULSC&A, MSS 339, b 21, f 19, H. E. Glenn to Thomas Shaw, September 14, 1953.

16   CULSC&A, MSS 339, b 21, f 19, Thomas Shaw to H. E. Glenn, September 25, 1956.

17   CULSC&A, S 339, b 21, f 19, H. E. Glenn to Thomas Shaw, October 23, 1956.

18   CULSC&A, S 339, b 21, f 19, H. E. Glenn to Thomas Shaw, October 23, 1956.

19   Turner, *Campus: An American Tradition*, 252.

20   Turner, *Campus: An American Tradition*, 260, 264; "Clemson Building Program Criticized," *Independent*, May 4, 1956, 21. In 1956 a report to the South Carolina General Assembly by its Fiscal Survey Commission expressed doubt that the expansion of physical facilities was wise. The report recommended that a Board of Control screen expenditures for new facilities and for renovations during the coming five years. The Task Force found the construction of new dormitories was expensive and "in our opinion do not compare favorably with new dormitory facilities at other state institutions." The report concluded that the new dormitory (Johnstone Hall) built by Daniel Construction Co. and "opened last year to replace the school's historic barracks" were "without any uniformity of plan or design with existing campus buildings . . . Older buildings at Clemson are put in unfair comparison with the nearby new construction and cause a bad impression for the institution." As a final observation the Task Force expressed concern over the "encroachment on the magnificent Clemson Campus which will result from construction of Hartwell Dam."("Clemson Building Program Criticized," *Independent*, May 4, 1956, 30–32.)

21   Cresap, McCormick, and Paget Management Engineers, *Clemson Agricultural College Survey of Administrative Management*, vol. 1 (New York: Cresap, McCormick, and Paget, 1955), sec. 5, 12; hereinafter cited as *CMP Report*. For an excellent analysis and summary, see Reel, *THS*, vol. 1, 412–19.

22   *CMP Report*, vol. 1, Chapter 2, 18.

23   Reel, *THS*, vol. 1, 412–13.

24   CULSC&A, S 87, b 47, f 13, Harlan McClure to R. C. Edwards, August 3, 1959; CULSC&A, S 11, f 435.

25   CULSC&A, S 87, b 47, f 13. Harlan McClure outlined the master plan of 1960 in his memo to President Edwards dated August 3, 1959. The master plan was to include area studies of each building group, external landscape development plans, a "Master Model" demountable by sections, and phasing diagrams. McClure drew up cost estimates for completing the plan, but no record of the plan exists; only the three-dimensional model was completed. The model was relocated to the east end of Lee Gallery in 1968. Its whereabouts after that move are unknown.

26   CULSC&A, S 30, *Periodic Reports to the Board of Trustees*, March 9, 1966, November 17, 1967.

27   Dober, *Campus Planning*, 147–48. The first college to set up a gymnasium was Harvard in 1826, when a dining hall was used for this purpose; a separate structure was erected circa 1840.

28   Reel, *THS*, vol. 1, 479–80.

29   CULSC&A, MSS 339, b 21, f 19, H. E. Glenn to C. E. Daniel, September 21, 1953.

30   CULSC&A, S 12, f 67, R. C. Edwards to Huger Sinkler, January 15, 1965.

31   "Coliseum Issue Rising Again," *Greenville News*, April 6, 1965, 4.

32   "New Governor, New Budget Confronts S. C. Legislators," *Independent*, April 27, 1965, 9.

33   CULSC&A, S 12, f 68, 2; *President's Report to the Board of Trustees*, May 28, 1985, 17.

34   CULSC&A, S 30, *President's Report to the Board of Trustees*, May 28, 1965; and Minutes, May 28, 1965, 181.

35   CULSC&A, S 12, f 67, Hassie Forrester to R. C. Edwards, May 3, 1965.

36   Wells, John E., "Sirrine, Joseph Emory (1872–1947)," North Carolina Architects and Builders: A Biographical Dictionary, 2009, https://ncarchitects.lib.ncsu.edu/people/P000303.

37   CULSC&A, S 12, f 67, William H. Wiley to J. K. Williams, June 1, 1965.

38   CULSC&A, S 12, f 67, R. C. Edwards to Mrs. Thomas B. Cooper, June 9, 1965. Edwards wrote: "Since we have not as yet determined what we will build and the cost and method of financing, it is impossible to fully answer your question about possible increases in student fees."

39   CULSC&A, S 83, b 22, f 9, Walter Cox to R. C. Edwards, July 6, 1965. Members of the committee included Walter Cox (Chair), Wright Bryan, Ralph Collins, Frank Howard, Harlan McClure, Robert Ritchie, E. P. Willimon, Melford Wilson, and Joe Young.

40   CULSC&A, S 83, b 22, f 9, Walter Cox to R. C. Edwards, July 6, 1965. The committee also recommended that the present field house be used for physical training and intramural programs when the intercollegiate athletic program was transferred to other facilities.

41   CULSC&A, S83, b 22, f 9, R. C. Edwards to Walter Cox, July 7, 1965.

42   CULSC&A, S83, b 22, f 9, R. C. Edwards to Building Committee for the Physical Recreation Building, July 10, 1965. Edwards appointed the members which consisted of Walter Cox, Harlan McClure, Joe Young, Melford Wilson, and Ralph Collins (Chair). No other documentation for this committee exists.

43   CULSC&A, S 12, f 67, Hassie Forrester to Building Committee, October 21, 1965.

44   CULSC&A, S 12, f 67, Hassie Forrester to Ralph Collins, October 22, 1965.

45   CULSC&A, S 12 f 67, Ralph Collins to Hassie Forrester, October 25, 1965.

46   "Plans for Coliseum Revealed," *The Tiger*, January 21, 1966, 3; CULSC&A, S 12, f 67, "Start of Clemson All-Purpose Coliseum Set for July," *Greenville News*, January 21, 1966.

47   CULSC&A, S 12, f 67, Charles L. Bates to R. C. Edwards, January 12, 1966.

48   "Plans for Coliseum Revealed," *The Tiger*, January 21, 1966, 3.

49   CULSC&A, S 12, f 67, Ralph Collins to Building Committee, October 28, 1965.

50   Bates interview, March 16, 2020. Ralph Collins was not pleased with the design.

51   CULSC&A, S12, f 67, Charles L. Bates to Ralph Collins, February 28, 1966.

52   CULSC&A, S 12, f 68, Ralph Collins to R. C. Edwards and Committee, May 27, 1966.

53   When asked about the metamorphic changes to his original design, Bates expressed no regret over the changes, only that the set budget made them necessary. Bates interview, March 16, 2020.

54   CULSC&A, S 12, f 68, Ralph Collins to R. C. Edwards and Committee, May 27, 1966.

55   CULSC&A, S 12, f 68, Charles L. Bates to Ken Naslund, May 11, 1966.

56   CULSC&A, S 12, f 68, Charles L. Bates to Ken Naslund, May 11, 1966.

57   CULSC&A, S 12, f 68, Ralph Collins to Building Committee, May 25, 1966.

58   CULSC&A, S 83, b22, f 9, R. C. Edwards to Wright Bryan, February 22, 1966.

59   CULSC&A, S 83, b22, f 10, Memoranda of Williamson and Bryan, August–September 1969. Campus maps of the period clearly show the growth in the number of parking areas on campus.

60   CULSC&A, S 87, b 47, f 13. The author of this proposal is not provided. The name of A. W. Rigsby, Comptroller, appears at the top. The last page bears the date of August 1969. No other records show the fate of the document; it is likely that Bryan's impending retirement precipitated its creation.

61   CULSC&A, S 83, b 22, f 10, Stan Nicholas to Harlan McClure, Sep. 1, 1970.

62   C. I. Gray, "Clemson Facility Needs More Funds," *Greenville News-Piedmont* (Greenville, SC), November 16, 1974, 17.

63   Gray, "Clemson Facility," 17; CULSC&A, S 13, f 141, R. C. Edwards to the Continuing Education Center Planning Committee, March 23, 1973.

64   CULSC&A, S 13, f 141, R. C. Edwards to the Continuing Education Center Planning Committee, March 23, 1973; CULSC&A, S 13, f 74, R. C. Edwards to John Weems, January 26, 1973.

65   CULSC&A, S 13, f 465, P. C. Smith to Heads of All State Agencies, May 4, 1973.

66   CULSC&A, S 13, f 74, John Weems to R. C. Edwards, January 23, 1973. Among those contacting Edwards were Hallman and Weems of Aiken, SC and Craig and Gaulden of Greenville. Weems, of the firm Hallman and Weems, wrote Edwards: "No doubt there are at least a dozen architectural firms in this state who would consider the commission for your continuing education center to be a real plum and no doubt a number of them have already contacted you. . . . We were not included in the last four state bonded projects for Clemson— and we understand why we were not; but we fervently hope we may be seriously considered for this Center."

67   CULSC&A, S 13, f 141, 142, Victor Hurst to R. C. Edwards, June 17, 1974. Edwards also polled his academic deans for ideas on programs to develop within the center. Although most colleges engaged in some sort of continuing education activities, they used only a small percentage of the total budget. See Wallace Trevillian's response to Edwards. At this time some continuing education programs were offered through the Clemson Area Continuing Education Center, an agency separate from the University. See also the objection raised by Dean Victor Hurst, CULSC&A, S 13, f 142.

68   CULSC&A, S 13, f 142, Minutes of the Building Committee for CEC, June 6, 1974.

69   CULSC&A, S 13, f 142, Minutes of the Building Committee for CEC, June 6, 1974.

70   CULSC&A, MSS A2015-005, b 12, Craig and Gaulden, "A Site

Evaluation Study for the Clemson University Continuing Education Center," August 1974, 3.

71   Earl Gatlin, "Master Planner—Advisor, Not Decision Maker," *The Tiger*, November 2, 1973, 10. Although Eflin referred to himself as "planner-advisor, not a decision maker," this self-assessment did not prevent him from recommending the destruction of numerous campus structures—including the Sheep Barn, Trustee House, and all pre-fab housing—in the name of better land use. He also recommended "limiting the grounds surrounding the Calhoun mansion" and making Bowman Field a parking lot because it was "no longer a source of entertainment." CULSC&A, S 87, b 47, f 14, Confidential memo, February 12, 1973.

72   Earl Gatlin, "Master Planner—Advisor, Not Decision Maker," *The Tiger*, November 2, 1973, 10; Debbie Graham, "Evolutionary Process Serves Clemson's Growing Needs," *The Tiger*, November 2, 1973, 11.

73   CULSC&A, S 37, Clemson University Subject Files, "Campus Planner Happiest with Pedestrian Routing," *Messenger*, February 8, 1973, 9A.

74   CULSC&A, S 35, b 5, f 48, R. C. Edwards to Kirk Craig, November 6, 1975; CULSC&A, A2015-005, b 12, Craig Gaulden Davis Records, Kirk Craig to Melford Wilson, December 29, 1975.

75   CULSC&A, S 35, b 5, f 48, R. C. Edwards to Kirk Craig, November 6, 1975; CULSC&A, A2015-005, b 12, Craig Gaulden Davis Records, Kirk Craig to Melford Wilson, December 29, 1975.

76   C. I. Gray, "Clemson Returns Money for Center," *Greenville News-Piedmont*, November 15, 1975, 1A.

77   CULSC&A, S 35, b 5, f 50, Stan Nicholas to Bill Atchley, August 23, 1979. Nicholas recommended the firm of Wilbur Smith and Associates.

78   CULSC&A, S 35, b 5, f 50, Laventhol & Horwath, "Market Study and Financial Projections for the Proposed 175-Room Continuing Education Center," October 1981.

79   CULSC&A, S 35, b 5, f 49, Atchley's statement to the South Carolina General Assembly [1981]. Atchley addressed the General Assembly asking the body to override the governor's veto of the continuing education center and the proposed Energy Research Center.

80   CULSC&A, S 30, "Report of the Board of Visitors," April 19, 1968 and April 29, 1969, found in the *President's Report to the Board of Trustees*.

81   Turner, *Campus*, 250.

82   CULSC&A, S 27, f 2–f 23, Speeches of Bill Atchley, 1980–81.

83   CULSC&A, S 27, b 3, f 29, Atchley remarks at Thurmond dinner, Greenville, August 20, 1982.

84   CULSC&A, S 27, b 3, f 26, Atchley address to Faculty, May 1982.

85   CULSC&A, S 35, b 5, f 49, Paul McAlister to Bill Atchley, September 10, 1982.

86   CULSC&A, S 35 b 5 f 49, Bill Atchley to Paul McAlister, November 5, 1982. Atchley outlined for McAlister "another philosophy" regarding financing, one that had been used successfully for many years at Santee Cooper. Atchley also remarked that he had studied an alternative financing proposal, "Preliminary Private Financing Alternatives for the Continuing Education Center" by Professor

Olgun Ersenkal in the Department of Planning Studies.

87   CULSC&A, S 78, b 25, f 1, Mark Wright to Harry Durham, December 7, 1982.

88   Harry Durham, Director Emeritus, University Relations, in discussion with the author, May 14, 2015.

89   CULSC&A, S 78, b 24, f 29, "Strom Thurmond Center Guidelines for Potential Developers," July 28, 1983.

90   CULSC&A, S 30, Minutes, January 27, 1984. The State Attorney General ruled that construction of the Strom Thurmond Institute and Center was subject to compliance with the South Carolina Consolidated Procurement Code. "As presently contemplated, the Center will consist of the STI building to house Senator Thurmond's papers and memorabilia, a performing arts center, and a continuing education center, *as well as a golf course and marina*" (author's emphasis).

91   CULSC&A, S 30, Minutes, January 27, 1984.

92   Kavin [sic] Taylor, "Institute Set Back," *The Tiger*, February 9, 1984, 11; CULSC&A, S 78, b 24, f 29; Paul Davidson, "Clemson May Build, Sell Campus Condos," *The State*, December 29, 1983, 1B.

93   CULSC&A, S 308, Office of Campus Planning, Minutes of the Planning Board, February 1984.

94   CULSC&A, S 308, Office of Campus Planning, Minutes of the Planning Board, February 1984.

95   James H. Boniface, *Clemson University Master Plan Site Analysis: the Strom Thurmond Center* (Clemson, SC: Clemson University, 1984).

96   "Consultant Invites Written Comments on Site Options for Thurmond Center," in *Clemson Newsletter* (Clemson, SC), April 2, 1984, 2.

97   CULSC&A, S 308. Office of Campus Planning, Schematic Design Review, April 1, 1985, 2, 4. The Planning Office recommended against putting balconies on the tower, given the "grandiose nature of the entire design" and cited that "the papal balcony effect" seemed "inappropriate."

98   "Senate Panel Oks Bond Bills; CU Institute Gets $5 Million," *Independent-Mail* (Anderson, SC), May 7, 1986, 6A.

99   "Riley Vetoes Arena, 4 Other Area Projects, Six Upstate Projects Eventually Will Benefit," *Independent-Mail*, June 19, 1986, 1A; Ed Miller, "Arena, Other Area Projects Saved as Lawmakers Override 41 Vetoes," *Independent-Mail*, June 20, 1986, 1A. Provost David Maxwell stated that the Strom Thurmond continuing education building would be a facility for classrooms and offices only.

100   Mark Schoen, "Architects Clean Up Thurmond Institute Design," *The Tiger*, April 3, 1987, 2.

101   See Richard P. Dober, *Campus Design* (New York: Wiley, 1992), 44–49 for an explanation of campus designs and growth patterns.

102   Dober, *Campus Planning*, 40. "American designers, in placing new buildings on old campuses, have preferred to have each building stand free from its neighbors, rather than tie the old to the new. As a result, many American campuses are diffused, amorphous, haphazard and collections of motley buildings." (Dober, *Campus Planning*, 40.)

103   Richard P. Dober, *Campus Landscape: Functions, Forms, Features* (New York: Wiley, 2000), 88; Dober, *Campus Planning*, 213.

CHAPTER THREE

1 Doris Betts, *Halfway Home and a Long Way to Go: The Report of the 1986 Commission on the Future of the South* (Research Triangle Park, NC: Southern Growth Policies Board, 1986), 20–24.

2 Clemson University, *The Second Century: A Partnership for Economic Progress through Academic Excellence* (Clemson, SC: Clemson University, 1989), 1–12.

3 CULSC&A, S 61, b 95, f 867, Minutes of the Facilities Planning Committee, August 26, 1992.

4 See Dober, *Campus Design*, 247 for characteristics of campus master plans of the time.

5 CULSC&A, S 83, b 22, f 9, Robert C. Edwards to Wright Bryan, February 22, 1966.

6 Dober, *Campus Design*, 227.

7 "Multistorey Car Park," Wikipedia, accessed November 16, 2016, https://en.wikipedia.org/wiki/Multistorey_car_park; Jane Holtz Kay, "A Brief History of Parking: The Life and Afterlife of Paving the Planet," *Architecture* 90, no. 2 (2001): 76–79, 122; Beth Broome, "1111 Lincoln Road," *Architectural Record* (June 19, 2010), https://www.architecturalrecord.com/articles/8232-lincoln-road.

8 *Clemson University Long Range Master Plan* (Clemson, SC: Clemson University, 1993), 67–68.

9 *Growth by Design: Clemson University Master Plan Summary Report* (Clemson, SC: Clemson University, 2003), 15.

10 Dober, *Campus Design*, 227: "If campus design were a theological statement, there would be only one deadly sin: the presence of parking in the wrong location."

11 *Growth by Design*, 15; CULSC&A, S 336, James F. Barker email to David Richardson, September 14, 2010. Richardson had written Barker to suggest building a parking garage below the soccer field. Gains in parking spaces were estimated at 1,500–3,500.

12 *Clemson University Botanical Garden Guide to Future Development* (Clemson, SC: Clemson University, 1990), 3.

13 CULSC&A, S 210, b 9, a 03-66, "Report Clemson Horticultural Gardens."

14 CULSC&A, S 210, b 9, a 03-66, Carl W. Helms to Benton H. Box, October 13, 1986. The project was titled "The Piedmont Environmental Science Museum," a terminal project in landscape architecture by Lell E. Barnes III.

15 *Clemson University Botanical Garden Guide*, 3.

16 *Clemson University Botanical Garden Guide*, 38.

17 *Clemson University Botanical Garden Guide*, 38.

18 *Clemson University Botanical Garden Guide*, 11.

19 *Clemson University Botanical Garden Guide*, 38.

20 *Clemson University Botanical Garden Guide*, 28. In November 2017 garden staff member John Bodiford escorted the author and Kathy Edwards to the proposed site.

21 *Clemson University Botanical Garden Guide*, 38.

22 CULSC&A, S 210, b 12, a 03-66, John Kelly to Gary Ransdell,

May 6, 1992.

23   CULSC&A, S 210, b 12, a 03-66, John Kelly to Gary Ransdell, July 10, 1991.

24   According to an unframed color rendering of the Botanical Garden Conservatory, CULSC&A.

25   John Kelly, "Director's Report, *Botanical Garden Quarterly* 1, no. 1 (1991): 5-6.

26   "Southern Exposure for State Government," *Inside Clemson*, November 17, 1995, 3.

27   "*Southern Living* Home Planned for Botanical Garden," *Inside Clemson*, November 29, 1996, 1.

28   Commission on the Future of Clemson University (CFC), *Final Report* (Clemson, SC: Clemson University, 1998), 6.

29   CFC, *Final Report*, 6.

30   CFC, *Final Report*, 31.

31   CFC, *Final Report*, 17–18.

32   Southern Education Foundation, *Miles to Go South Carolina* (Atlanta, GA: Southern Education Foundation, 2002), ix.

33   Southern Education Foundation, *Miles to Go South Carolina*, 7.

34   CULSC&A, S 336, b 43, f 694, James F. Barker to Darla Moore, June 30, 2000.

35   Patricia Sellers, "Don't Mess with Darla," *Fortune*, September 8, 1997, https://fortune.com/1997/09/08/darla-moore-richard-rainwater/.

36   Ann Paisley Chandler, "Darla Moore," *Philanthropy NYU*, Winter 2013, accessed November 17, 2016, www.philanthropynyu.com.

37   Chandler, "Darla Moore."

38   "There Is Nothing Worse Than Unrealized Promise" and "Clemson's Promise: To Be the State's Leader in Learner-centered Education Reform," unpublished documents, October 14, 1999, 13. Documents received from Neill Cameron (Vice-president Emeritus, Clemson University Office for Development) via Joyce Ogg (Alumni Development Manager, Clemson University) September 19, 2016.

39   Neill Cameron (Vice-president Emeritus, Clemson University Office for Development), in discussion with author, March 22, 2016.

40   Chandler, "Darla Moore."

41   CFC, *Final Report*, 40.

42   *Growth by Design*, 1.

43   Thomas & Denzinger Architects and Payette Associates, *Center of Centers Master Plan* (Clemson, SC: Clemson University, 2003) 18–20, https://cufacilities.sites.clemson.edu/documents/planning/Center%20of%20Centers%20Master%20Plan%202003.pdf; "Highlights," *Clemson World*, Spring 2003, 24. Professor Emeritus John Jacques developed the original idea for the Center of Centers.

44   *Growth by Design*, 1.

45   Some of the buildings constructed were the Brooks Center for the Performing Arts, the Madren Conference Center, the Fluor-Daniel Engineering Innovation Building, the Godley-Snell Animal Science Building, the McFadden Athletics Building, the Hendrix Student Center, and four dormitories.

46   Ben Sill, "CURIOUS Campus: An Academic Showplace," [2006], 1; seven-page document obtained from Ben Sill (Professor Emeritus, Civil Engineering, Clemson University).

47   Sill, "CURIOUS Campus," 1.

48   Sill, "CURIOUS Campus," 1. An earlier proposal to create a "retirement village" occurred in the 1970s when David Fleming, director of Institutional Research, put forward a facility that would have been run and administered by Clemson students, and would have provided work and training for nursing and business students. Provost Emerita Doris Helms, in discussion with author, March 24, 2016.

49   Sill, "CURIOUS Campus," 2.

50   Kathy Kuneyl, Richard Massingill, Kelly Miller, and Christopher Walsh, "CURIOUS Campus," n.d., 3. Six-page document obtained from Ben Sill (Professor Emeritus, Civil Engineering, Clemson University).

51   Sill, "CURIOUS Campus," 1.

52   Sill, "CURIOUS Campus," Section II, 3.

53   Thomas W. Norwood, "Upstate University Has Strong Ties to Lowcountry," *News and Courier/Evening Post* (Charleston, SC), April 3, 1988, 1B. Barker developed the idea for the center after he visited Charleston during his tenure as a professor at Mississippi State University and observed that Charleston's urban environment would allow students the opportunity to trace the evolution of buildings to learn "the best of what the past offered in design and function . . . and . . . new ways to design buildings that fit into the existing streetscape without slavishly copying the past."

54   Allison L. Bruce, "Expanding on a School," *Post and Courier*, December 4, 2001, 1D. The Center planned to move from Bull Street to the third and fourth floors of the former water works building on 14 George Street, also known as the Middleton-Pinckney House, and share the house with other tenants: Spoleto Festival USA (the main office of Charleston's annual music and arts festival) and the Charleston Symphony Orchestra. However, because of damage caused by Hurricane Hugo in 1989, the Center moved instead to new quarters on Franklin Street.

55   Bruce, "Expanding," 1D. Two proposals to create a center for design and the arts, and another for a center for urban design would have located the center in the lot directly behind Spoleto Festival USA; CULSC&A, S 336, b 30, f 468, Presidential Records of James F. Barker. In April 2001 a memorandum of understanding outlined the specifics of the agreement involving the City of Charleston, Spoleto Festival USA, and Clemson University. By September 2002, per terms of that memorandum, Clemson exercised its option to build the new facility at 11 and/or 13 George Street.

56   CULSC&A, S 336, b 30, f 468, Presidential Records of James F. Barker; Tenisha Waldo, "Clemson's Lowcountry Center for Architecture to Honor Paolozzi," *Post and Courier*, July 23, 2005, 3B. The Countess, also a race car driver, philanthropist, and patron of the arts, had established the Spaulding Paolozzi Foundation to support efforts concerning the environment, the sustainability of agriculture, and issues involving the elderly and women. "Alicia Spaulding Paolozzi," Historic Saranac Lake Wiki, accessed September 20, 2016, http://localwiki.org/hsl/Alicia_Spaulding_Paolozzi.

57   CULSC&A, S 336, b 30, f 469, Ross Norton, "Five Finalists Named in International Design Competition for Clemson Architecture Center in Charleston," November 19, 2004; "News Digest," *Inside*

Clemson, December 2004, 2.

58   CULSC&A, S 336, b 30, f 469, Ross Norton, "Five Finalists Named in International Design Competition for Clemson Architecture Center in Charleston," November 19, 2004; "News Digest," *Inside Clemson*, December 2004, 2; Robert Behre, "Design for New Center to Get Input from Public," *Post and Courier*, January 3, 2005, 1B; "Clemson Names Firm to Design Charleston Architecture Center," *Inside Clemson*, Feb. 2005, 1.

59   Robert Behre, "Clemson Center Design Opens Rift," *Post and Courier*, January 24, 2005, 1B; Robert Behre, "Hard Road Ahead for Center," *Post and Courier*, July 18, 2005, 1B.

60   Behre, "Hard Road," 1B.

61   Behre, "Hard Road," 1B..

62   James F. Barker, "Clemson Welcomes Community Input on Its Architecture Center," *Post and Courier*, November 20, 2005, 11A. The opposing view is presented by Frank Brumley and Katharine Robinson, in "Historic Foundation Says Building 'Unacceptable,'" *Post and Courier*, November 20, 2005, 11A.

63   Barker, "Clemson Welcomes Community Input on Its Architecture Center," 11A. One public forum, a lecture by architect Kenneth Schwartz of the University of Virginia, dealt with the role of contemporary architecture in historic settings.

64   "Historic Foundation's Good Reasons to Redesign or Move Clemson Center," *Post and Courier*, November 20, 2005, 10A.

65   Robert Behre, "Clemson Trustees Approve Land Buy: Meeting Street Tract Would Be Site of Proposed Architecture Center," *Post and Courier*, October 10, 2006, 3B; Robert Behre, "Clemson Announces New Architects for Its New Meeting Street Building," *Post and Courier*, February 16, 2012, https://www.postandcourier.com/clemson-announces-new-architects-for-its-new-meeting-street-building/article_d4f428d0-91cf-5c6d-9061-ec9b74555d30.html. The site contained a single house, which was to be preserved, and a one-story brick office building, which was slated for demolition.

66   Behre, "Clemson Announces New Architects for Its New Meeting Street Building," *Post and Courier*, February 16, 2012; Robert Behre, "Clemson Plans Architecture Site in Downtown Charleston," *Post and Courier*, February 20, 2012.

67   Behre, "Clemson Announces New Architects for Its New Meeting Street Building,"; Behre, "Clemson Plans Architecture Site in Downtown Charleston."

68   Robert Behre, "Clemson Architecture Center Design Gets Charleston's Stamp of Approval, Design of Clemson's New Architecture Building Up for Preliminary Approval," *Post and Courier*, June 24, 2014, https://www.postandcourier.com/archives/clemson-architecture-center-design-gets-charlestons-stamp-of-approval-design-of-clemsons-new-architecture-building/article_a7b0b861-8b1f-58e4-9612-42fa45d45713.html; Robert Behre, "Clemson Architecture Center Gets City Approval, Residents Pan Design," *Post and Courier*, June 25, 2014. Some said the holes in the aluminum screen, referred to by some as "a pigeon pen," would have allowed birds to nest in them. Cloepfil responded by changing the design to a 45-degree slant so that birds could not roost.

69   Paul Bowers, "Talking Contemporary Design and the Clemson Architecture Center with Brad Cloepfil," *Charleston City Paper* (Charleston, SC), October 16, 2013, https://www.charlestoncitypaper.com/story/talking-contemporary-design-and-the-clemson-architecture-center-with-brad-cloepfil?oid=4779384.

70   Behre, "Stamp of Approval."

71   Robert Behre, "Charleston Groups Sue Over Approval of Clemson Architecture Center's Proposed Design," *Post and Courier*, July 24, 2014; Charleston County Court of Common Pleas, Case no. 2014CP1004531, accessed June 2020, https://jcmsweb. charlestoncounty.org/PublicIndex/PISearch.aspx.

72   "Complaint, Petition and Notice of Intent to Appeal," July 23, 2014, Case no. 2014CP1004531, 8, accessed June 2020, https:// jcmsweb.charlestoncounty.org/PublicIndex/PISearch.aspx.

73   "Complaint, Petition and Notice of Intent to Appeal."

74   Behre, "Charleston Groups Sue."

75   "Consent Order of Dismissal," December 5, 2014, Case no. 2014CP1005431, Charleston County Court of Common Pleas, accessed August 2020, https://jcmsweb.charlestoncounty.org/ PublicIndex/PISearch.aspx.

76   Robert Behre, "Cigar Factory to House CU Center," *Post and Courier*, January 20, 2016, https://www.postandcourier.com/ business/cigar-factory-to-house-cu-center/article_dd965541-49ec-5c84-9e43-21cf55d2053e.html; Robert Behre, "Clemson Programs Find a Home," *Post and Courier*, November 22, 2016, B1; Bryce Donovan, "Clemson Design Center Officially Opens Its Doors in Charleston," Clemson University, August 25, 2016, https://newsstand. clemson.edu/mediarelations/clemson-design-center-officially-opens-its-doors-in-charleston/. State Representative Harry B. "Chip" Limehouse III, chair of the House Ways and Means subcommittee on higher education, urged Clemson to reconsider the design. John M. McDermott, "Clemson Wants Local Architecture Programs Under One Roof," *Post and Courier*, July 16, 2015, https://www. postandcourier.com/business/clemson-wants-local-architecture-programs-under-1-roof/article_8591f823-2604-5dc8-849c-ba8179a0079b.html; Robert Behre, "Clemson Dropping Modern Plan for Building," *Post and Courier*, November 18, 2014, https:// www.postandcourier.com/archives/clemson-dropping-modern-plan-for-building/article_573377f8-817c-52cc-91a4-76973dacf12f. html. See also the editorial "Clemson Sees the Design Light," *Post and Courier*, November 20, 2014, A12, https://www.postandcourier.com/ opinion/clemson-sees-the-design-light/article_cc1f0fca-18c6-55ce-999f-f2c4968e19cb.html. Other buildings in Charleston generated opposition and debate through the years: for example, the Charleston Gateway Center at Calhoun and East Bay, one of the first buildings to use metal louvers; a small modern home on Prices Alley; the demolition of the Mendel Rivers Building at Charlotte and Meeting streets; and the Addelstone Library of the College of Charleston with its revolving doors, expanses of glass, and concrete cylinders.

77   "Cigar Factory," Wikipedia, accessed December 5, 2016, https:// en.wikipedia.org/wiki/Cigar_Factory. In the 1940s, the factory was the location of the civil rights strike where the anthem "We Shall Overcome" emerged.

78   Donovan, "Clemson Design Center;" Robert Behre, "New Clemson Architecture Center Offers Several Big Lessons," *Post and Courier*, November 13, 2016, E1, https://www.postandcourier.com/ columnists/new-clemson-architecture-center-offers-several-big-lessons/article_db46ebe6-a762-11e6-acce-87771a140696.html.

79   James F. Barker, quoted in CAAH, *The Vision for the Center for Visual Arts* (Clemson, SC: CAAH, Clemson University, n.d.), n.p. Spiral-bound publication obtained from Denise Woodward-Detrich (Director, Lee Gallery, Clemson University), December 2016.

80   Boudreaux Group, *The Center for Visual Arts at Clemson University Feasibility Study* (Columbia, SC: Boudreaux Group,

2008), 9. Obtained from Denise Woodward-Detrich (Director, Lee Gallery, Clemson University), December 2016.

81   Boudreaux Group, *Feasibility Study*, 13.

82   Boudreaux Group, *Feasibility Study*, 13.

83   The four schemes are fully explained and illustrated in The Boudreaux Group, *Feasibility Study*, 29–37.

84   Boudreaux Group, *Feasibility Study*, 30.

85   Boudreaux Group, *Feasibility Study*, 27.

86   Boudreaux Group, *Feasibility Study*, 30.

87   CULSC&A, S 336, b 29, f 449, James F. Barker to Ben Rook, November 22, 2002.

88   The Boudreaux Group, *Feasibility Study*, 39–54.

89   The Boudreaux Group, *Feasibility Study*, 49.

90   CULSC&A, S 336, Center for Visual Arts, oversize drawing by Thomas Phifer, n.d.

91   The Boudreaux Group, *Feasibility Study*, 56.

92   "Highlights," *Clemson World* (Clemson, SC: Clemson University, 2003), 24.

93   [Neill Cameron], "The Clemson Experience (A Clemson Icon)," PowerPoint presentation, n.d.; Cameron interview.

94   [Cameron], "The Clemson Experience"; Cameron interview.

95   [Cameron], "The Clemson Experience"; Cameron interview.

96   Brian Duigan, "Financial Crisis of 2007–2008," Britannica, accessed February 21, 2020, https://www.britannica.com/event/financial-crisis-of-2007-2008/Effects-and-aftermath-of-the-crisis; "Subprime Mortgage Crisis," Wikipedia, accessed December 1, 2016, https://en.wikipedia.org/wiki/Subprime_mortgage_crisis.

97   South Carolina Department of Commerce, Research Division, *South Carolina Economic Indicator Report* (Columbia: South Carolina Department of Commerce, 2010), 3, https://dc.statelibrary.sc.gov/bitstream/handle/10827/27510/DOC_Economic_Indicator_Report_2010-06.pdf.

98   Wayne Washington, "State Bans Some Colleges from New Construction," *The State*, September 30, 2010.

99   Rudolph Bell, "EXPERIENCE CLEMSON: How Clemson Is Waving Orange Along Main Street in Greenville," *Greenville News*, August 3, 2015, https://www.heraldonline.com/news/state/south-carolina/article29914207.html.

EPILOGUE

1   A gymnasium, first proposed in the 1890s, was not built until 1930; a student memorial chapel, proposed in the 1990s, was begun in 2019 thanks to the generosity of donors.

2   Saraswat, "Unbuilt Architecture."

BIBLIOGRAPHY

ARCHIVAL SOURCES

CLEMSON UNIVERSITY

SPECIAL COLLECTIONS AND ARCHIVES

UNIVERSITY ARCHIVES
Series 1, Enoch W. Sikes Presidential Records, 1925–31
Series 2, Enoch W. Sikes Presidential Records, 1931–41
Series 7, Robert F. Poole Presidential Records, Committee Files, 1930–55
Series 11, Robert C. Edwards Presidential Records, 1958–65
Series 12, Robert C. Edwards Presidential Records, 1966–70
Series 13, Robert C. Edwards Presidential Records, 1960–79
Series 17, Walter M. Riggs Presidential Records, 1907–25
Series 18, Patrick H. Mell Presidential Records, 1902–09
Series 19, Bill Lee Atchley Presidential Records, 1971–86
Series 20, Bill Lee Atchley Presidential Records, 1974–85
Series 27, Bill Lee Atchley Presidential Speeches, 1979–85
Series 30, Board of Trustees Records, 1888–91
Series 35, Walter T. Cox Presidential Records, 1970–89
Series 37, Clemson University Subject Files
Series 38, Clemson University Biography Files
Series 61, A. Max Lennon Presidential Records, 1939–93
Series 78, Office of University Relations Records, 1965–96
Series 83, College of Architecture, Office of the Dean Records, 1940–88
Series 87, Vice-President for Business and Finance Records, 1900–2000
Series 100, Clemson University Photographs Collection
Series 102, Philip H. Prince Presidential Records, 1991–96
Series 103, A. Max Lennon Presidential Records, 1978–94
Series 104, Constantine W. Curris Presidential Records, 1979–2001
Series 210, School of Public Service and Agriculture Records
Series 308, Office of Campus Planning Records, 1996–2000
Series 312, Office for Development Records, 1960–2000
Series 336, James F. Barker Presidential Records, 1999–2013

MANUSCRIPTS
MSS 41, Rudolph Edward Lee Papers
MSS 80, Benjamin Ryan Tillman Papers
MSS 339, Charles Daniel Papers
A2015-005, Craig Gaulden Davis Records

PUBLICATIONS
Annual Report of the Trustees of the Clemson Agricultural College to the General Assembly of South Carolina (Columbia, SC: State Printer, 1890–1910)
Botanical Garden Newsletter (1990–99)
Clemson College: Its Past and Future (1954)
Clemson Newsletter (1984–85)
Clemson World (2003)
Inside Clemson (1995–96, 2004–05)
The Tiger (1914, 1941–51, 1966–87)

CAMPUS PLANNING DOCUMENTS

CLEMSON UNIVERSITY

An Atlas of Clemson College Properties. Clemson, SC: Clemson Agricultural College of South Carolina, 1945.
Boniface, James H. *Clemson University Master Plan Site Analysis: East Campus Student Activities Center*. Clemson, SC: Clemson University, 1985.
———. *Clemson University Master Plan Site Analysis: The Strom Thurmond Center*. Clemson, SC: Clemson University, 1984.
Boudreaux Group. *The Center for Visual Arts at Clemson University Feasibility Study*. Columbia, SC: Boudreaux

Group, 2008.

Clemson University Botanical Garden Guide to Future Development. Clemson, SC: Clemson University, 1990.

Clemson University Campus Master Plan. Clemson, SC: Clemson University, 1981.

Clemson University Campus Master Plan. Clemson, SC: Clemson University, 1992.

Clemson University Campus Master Plan. Clemson, SC: Clemson University, 2002.

Clemson University Comprehensive Master Plan. Phase 1: Survey. Interim Report on Existing Conditions and Programs. Clemson, SC: Clemson University, 1981.

Clemson University Comprehensive Master Plan Summary Report. Clemson, SC: Clemson University, 1981.

Clemson University High Ground Precinct Master Plan, vol. II. Clemson, SC: Clemson University, 2003.

Clemson University Long-Range Framework Plan. Clemson, SC: Clemson University, 2017, https://cufacilities.sites.clemson.edu/documents/planning/LRFP_lowres.pdf.

Clemson University Long Range Master Plan. Clemson, SC: Clemson University, 1993.

Clemson University Plan and Guidelines for Restoration, Rehabilitation and Maintenance of Historic Resources. Clemson, SC: Clemson University, 1995.

Clemson University Campus Planning Task Force. *Clemson University Long-range Framework Plan*. Clemson, SC: Clemson University, 2017.

Clemson University College of Architecture, Arts and Humanities, Department of Planning and Landscape Architecture. *Campus Preservation and Clemson Historic Resources: Seminar Proceedings*. Clemson, SC: Clemson University, 1995.

Growth by Design: Clemson University Master Plan Summary Report. Clemson, SC: Clemson University, 2003.

John Milner Associates, Inc. *Clemson University Preservation Master Plan*. Philadelphia, PA: John Milner Associates, 2009.

Perry, Shaw and Hepburn, Kehoe and Dean, Architects. *Clemson College Campus Master Plan*. Boston, MA: PSHKD, 1954.

Thomas & Denzinger Architects and Payette Associates. *Center of Centers Master Plan*. Clemson, SC: Clemson University, 2003, https://cufacilities.sites.clemson.edu/documents/planning/Center%20of%20Centers%20Master%20Plan%202003.pdf.

ARCHIVAL SOURCES

OTHER INSTITUTIONS

Agnes Scott College Archives, Photographs and Maps Collection.

Furman University Special Collections and Archives, Papers of President John L. Plyler.

Georgia Institute of Technology, Archives.

———. Facilities Department Drawings Collection.

———. Institutional Drawings Collection.

———. Early Presidents Collection.

Winthrop University Louise Pettus Archives and Special Collections, Photograph Collection.

SECONDARY SOURCES

ARTICLES

Abramson, Daniel M. "Stakes of the Unbuilt." *The Aggregate*, February 2, 2014, http://we-aggregate.org/piece/stakes-of-the-unbuilt.

"Alicia Spaulding Paolozzi." Historic Saranac Lake Wiki, accessed September 20, 2016, http://localwiki.org/hsl/Alicia_Spaulding_Paolozzi.

Anderson, Carol. "Log House on Campus Was Once Lodging Place for Travelers." *Messenger* (Clemson, SC), August 31, 1967, 17.

Besner, Linda. "Once in a Blue Moon: What We Can Learn from Things that Never Happened." *The Globe and Mail* (Toronto, ON), August 9, 2019, https://www.theglobeandmail.com/opinion/article-once-in-a-blue-moon-what-we-can-learn-from-things-that-never-happened/.

Bowers, Paul "Talking Contemporary Design and the Clemson Architecture Center with Brad Cloepfil." *Charleston City Paper* (Charleston, SC), October 16, 2013, https://www.charlestoncitypaper.com/story/talking-contemporary-design-and-the-clemson-architecture-center-with-brad-cloepfil?oid=4779384.

Broome, Beth. "1111 Lincoln Road." *Architectural Record*, June 19, 2010, https://www.architecturalrecord.com/articles/8232-lincoln-road.

Chandler, Ann Paisley. "Darla Moore." *Philanthropy NYU*, Winter 2013. Accessed November 17, 2016, www.philanthropynyu.com.

"Cigar Factory." Wikipedia, accessed December 5, 2016, https://en.wikipedia.org/wiki/Cigar_Factory.

"Clemson Experimental Forest." Wikipedia, accessed September 29, 2016, https://en.wikipedia.org/wiki/Clemson_Experimental_Forest.

Curtis, Wayne. "How Mayor Joe Riley Shaped Charleston." *Architect Magazine*, November 3, 2015, https://www.architectmagazine.com/design/how-mayor-joe-riley-shaped-charleston_o.

Donovan, Bryce. "Clemson Design Center Officially Opens Its Doors in Charleston." Clemson University, August 25, 2016, https://newsstand.clemson.edu/mediarelations/clemson-design-center-officially-opens-its-doors-in-charleston/

Duigan, Brian. "Financial Crisis of 2007–2008." Britannica, accessed February 21, 2020, https://www.britannica.com/event/financial-crisis-of-2007-2008/Effects-and-aftermath-of-the-crisis.

Funderburke, Richard D. "Bruce and Morgan." New Georgia Encyclopedia, December 7, 2016, https://www.georgiaencyclopedia.org/articles/arts-culture/bruce-and-morgan.

"George Parker Dead." *New York Times*, September 14, 1926, 29.

"Hanover House (Clemson)." Wikipedia, accessed April 23, 2019, https://en.wikipedia.org/wiki/Hanover_House_(Clemson).

"Historical Enrollment at a Glance (1900–2010)." Clemson University, accessed April 30, 2020, https://www.clemson.edu/institutional-effectiveness/documents/oir/historical/Historical-Enrollment-Detail.pdf.

Kay, Jane Holtz. "A Brief History of Parking: The Life and Afterlife of Paving the Planet." *Architecture* 90, no. 2 (2001): 76–79, 122.

Kelly, John. "Director's Report." *Botanical Garden Quarterly* 1, no. 1 (1991): 5-6.

"Multistorey Car Park," Wikipedia, accessed November 16, 2016, https://en.wikipedia.org/wiki/Multistorey_car_park.

Olmstead, Frederick Law. "How Not to Establish an Agricultural College." *The Nation* 3, no. 69 (1866): 335–36.

"Perry Dean Rogers Architects." Wikipedia, accessed January 10, 2017, https://en.wikipedia.org/wiki/Perry_Dean_Rogers_Architects.

Saraswat, Anupriya. "Unbuilt Architecture—UnBuilt Seeks to Celebrate Not Only What Could Have Been, But Also What We Will Leave Behind." Architecture Live!, accessed March 3, 2020, https://architecturelive.in/unbuilt-architecture-unbuilt-seeks-to-celebrate-not-only-what-could-have-been-but-also-what-we-will-leave-behind/.

Sellers, Patricia. "Don't Mess with Darla." *Fortune*, September 8, 1997, https://fortune.com/1997/09/08/darla-moore-richard-rainwater/.

"Subprime Mortgage Crisis." Wikipedia, accessed December 1, 2016, https://en.wikipedia.org/wiki/Subprime_mortgage_crisis.

Thomas, Rhondda. "Reconstruction, Public Memory, and the Making of Clemson University on John C. Calhoun's Fort Hill Plantation." *American Literary History* 30, no. 3 (2018): 584–607.

Vivian, Daniel. "Kelsey and Guild," in Walter Edgar, ed., *South Carolina Encyclopedia*. Columbia: University of South Carolina Press, 2006, 515–16.

Wells, John E. "Sirrine, Joseph Emory (1872–1947)." North Carolina Architects and Builders: A Biographical Dictionary, 2009, https://ncarchitects.lib.ncsu.edu/people/P000303.

BOOKS

Benjamin, Laura. *Clemson University College of Engineering: One Hundred Years of Progress*. Clemson, SC: Clemson University, 1989.

Bryan, Wright. *Clemson: An Informal History of the University, 1889–1979*. Columbia: R. L. Bryan, 1979.

Coulson, Jonathan, Paul Roberts, and Isabelle Taylor. *University Planning and Architecture: The Search for Perfection*. New York: Routledge, 2011.

Dober, Richard P. *Campus Design*. New York: Wiley, 1992.

———. *Campus Landscape: Functions, Form, Features*. New York: Wiley, 2000.

———. *Campus Planning*. New York: Reinhold, 1963.

Ferguson, Niall, ed. *Virtual History: Alternatives and Counterfactuals*. New York: Basic Books, 1999.

Grubiak, Margaret M. *White Elephants on Campus: The Decline of the University Chapel in America, 1920–1960*. Notre Dame, IN: University of Notre Dame Press, 2014.

Jones, Will. *Unbuilt Masterworks of the 21st Century: Inspirational Architecture for the Digital Age*. New York: Thames and Hudson, 2009.

Klauder, Charles Z. and Herbert C. Wise. *College Architecture in America*. New York: Charles Scribner's Sons, 1929.

Laurence, Peter L. *100 Years of Clemson Architecture: Southern Roots + Global Reach*. Clemson, SC: Clemson University Digital Press, 2013.

McKale, Donald M. and Jerome V. Reel, Jr., eds. *Tradition: A History of the Presidency of Clemson University*. Macon, GA: Mercer University Press, 1998.

Olmsted, Frederick Law. *A Few Things to Be Thought of Before Proceeding to Plan Buildings for the National Agricultural Colleges*. New York: American News Company, 1866.

Peterson, Jon A. *The Birth of City Planning in the United States, 1840–1917*. Baltimore: Johns Hopkins University Press, 2003.

Reel, Jerome V. Jr. *The High Seminary*, 2 vols. Clemson, SC: Clemson University Digital Press, 2011, 2013.

Russell, Ann R. *Legacy of a Southern Lady: Anna Calhoun Clemson, 1817–1875*. Clemson, SC: Clemson University Digital Press, 2007.

Schaffer, Alan. *Visions: Clemson's Yesteryears, 1880s–1960s*. Louisville, KY: Harmony House, 1990.

Sky, Alison and Michelle Stone. *Unbuilt America: Forgotten Architecture in the United States from Thomas Jefferson to the Space Age*. New York: McGraw-Hill, 1976.

Turner, Paul Venable. *Campus: An American Tradition*. Cambridge, MA: MIT Press, 1984.

———. *Academy Hill: The Andover Campus 1778 to the Present*. Andover, MA: Addison Gallery of American Art, Phillips Academy, 2000.

Wood, Loren M. *Beautiful Land of the Sky: John Muir's Forgotten Eastern Counterpart, Harlan P. Kelsey, Pioneering Our Native Plants and Eastern National Parks.* Bloomington, IN: iUniverse, 2013.

GOVERNMENT DOCUMENTS

Acts and Joint Resolutions of the General Assembly of the State of South Carolina. Columbia, SC: State Printer, 1900, accessed via https://babel.hathitrust.org.

Case records, Charleston County Court of Common Pleas, Case no. 2014CP1004531, 2014, accessed via https://jcmsweb.charlestoncounty.org/PublicIndex/PISearch.aspx.

Fiscal Survey Commission. *State Institutions of Higher Learning: Report No. 3 to the General Assembly of the State of South Carolina*, 1956.

INTERVIEWS (UNRECORDED)

Askew, George (Vice-President for Public Service and Agriculture, Clemson University), April 22, 2016.

Barker, James F. (President Emeritus, Clemson University), June 30, 2015.

Bates, Charles L. (Architect), March 17, 2020.

Bodiford, John (Senior Horticulturist, South Carolina Botanical Garden), October 31, 2017.

Bradshaw, David (Director Emeritus, Clemson University Horticultural Garden), September 23, 2019.

Cameron, Neill (Vice-President for Development, Clemson University), March 22, 2016.

Durham, Harry (Director Emeritus, University Relations, Clemson University), May 4, 2015.

Ellis, Clifford (Professor, City Planning and Real Estate Development, Clemson University), February 18, 2016.

Helms, Doris (Vice-President for Academic Affairs and Provost Emerita, Clemson University), March 14, 2016.

Hiott, William D. (Director, Historic Properties, Clemson University), August 11, 2016.

Jacques, John D. (Professor Emeritus of Architecture, Clemson University), May 27, 2015.

Reel, Jerome V. (Professor Emeritus and University Historian, Clemson University), October 1, 2014.

Russell, Ann (Independent scholar; former Curator of Fort Hill), December 15, 2015.

Sill, Ben (Professor Emeritus of Civil Engineering, Clemson University), October 8, 2014.

Vander Mey, Gerald (Director, University Planning and Design, Clemson University), February 6, 2015; Aug. 11, 2017.

NEWSPAPERS

Independent and *Independent-Mail*, Anderson, SC (1941–65, 1986)

News and Courier, News and Courier/Evening Post, and *Post and Courier*, Charleston, SC (1904, 1988, 2000–16)

Greenville News and *Greenville News-Piedmont*, Greenville, SC (1948–66, 1974–75, 2015)

The State, Columbia, SC (1904, 1983, 2010)

REPORTS

Betts, Doris. *Halfway Home and a Long Way to Go: The Report of the 1986 Commission on the Future of the South.* Research Triangle Park, NC: Southern Growth Policies Board, 1986.

[Cameron, Neill]. "The Clemson Experience (A Clemson Icon)." PowerPoint presentation, n.d.

Clemson University. *The Second Century: A Partnership for Economic Progress through Academic Excellence.* Clemson, SC: Clemson University, 1990.

College of Architecture, Arts and Humanities, Clemson University. *The Vision for the Center for Visual Arts*. Clemson, SC: Clemson University, n.d.

Commission on the Future of Clemson University. *Final Report*, Clemson, SC: Clemson University, 1998.

Commissioner of Agriculture, Commerce and Industries of the State of South Carolina. *Ninth Annual Report*. Columbia, SC: Gonzales and Bryan, State Printers, 1912.

Cresap, McCormick, and Paget Management Engineers. *Clemson Agricultural College Survey of Administrative Management*, vol. 1 (New York: Cresap, McCormick, and Paget, 1955).

Kelsey and Guild Landscape Architects. *Beautifying and Improving Greenville, South Carolina: Report to the Municipal League of Greenville, South Carolina*. Boston, MA: Kelsey and Guild, 1907.

——— . *The Improvement of Columbia, South Carolina: Report to the Civic League*. Columbia, SC: Kelsey and Guild, 1905.

Sill, Benjamin. "CURIOUS Campus: An Academic Showplace." 2006.

South Carolina Department of Commerce, Research Division. *South Carolina Economic Indicator Report*. Columbia: South Carolina Department of Commerce, 2010, https://dc.statelibrary.sc.gov/bitstream/handle/10827/27510/DOC_Economic_Indicator_Report_2010-06.pdf.

Southern Education Foundation, *Miles to Go South Carolina*. Atlanta, GA: Southern Education Foundation, 2002.

Triad Architectural Associates. *Existing Facilities Study Winthrop College*. Columbus, OH: Triad Architectural Associates, 1980.

Vander Mey, Gerald. *Interfaith Memorial Chapel Facility Program*. Clemson, SC: Clemson University, 2009.

UNPUBLISHED WORKS

"Clemson's Promise: To Be the State's Leader in Learner-centered Education Reform." Unpublished document. October 14, 1999.

Drury, Warren E., III. "The Architectural Development of Georgia Tech." Unpublished MA thesis, Georgia Institute of Technology, 1984.

Jones, Todd. "A History of Keney Park." Unpublished manuscript, 2011, https://www.gchartford.org/keney_park/History%20of%20Keney%20Park.pdf.

Kuneyl, Kathy, Richard Massingill, Kelly Miller, and Christopher Walsh. "CURIOUS Campus." n.d.

Thacker, Marta Leslie. "Working for the City Beautiful: Civic Improvement in Three South Carolina Communities." Unpublished MA thesis, University of South Carolina, 1999.

"There Is Nothing Worse Than Unrealized Promise." Unpublished document. October 14, 1999.

Printed in the USA
CPSIA information can be obtained
at www.ICGtesting.com
LVHW061059161123

764122LV00010BA/18

9781949979626